Masonry and Medieval Mysticism

Traces of a Hidden Tradition

by
Isabel Cooper-Oakley

THEOSOPHICAL PUBLISHING HOUSE LTD
68 Great Russell Street London WC1B 3BU

ADYAR-INDIA   WHEATON ILL.-USA

First Published 1900
Second Edition 1977

ISBN 7229 5053 5 (case)
ISBN 7229 5054 3 (paper)

CONTENTS.

		PAGE
I.	INTRODUCTION	5
II.	TOWARDS THE HIDDEN SOURCES OF MASONRY	31
III.	THE TRADITIONS OF THE KNIGHTS TEMPLARS REVIVED IN MASONRY	76
IV.	THE TROUBADOURS	103
V.	THE HEAVENLY KINGDOM OF THE HOLY GRAIL	137

INTRODUCTION.

THE series of sketches which are now brought together appeared originally as detached articles in the pages of the *Theosophical Review*, written, however, with the object of demonstrating to students of Theosophy that a definite design could be traced beneath the apparently disconnected mystic doctrines held by the many occult brotherhoods, heretic sects and mystic associations which cluster so thickly together as we glance along the historical by-ways of religious thought during the Middle Ages. That object becomes clearer when they appear as they do now in closer juxtaposition.

To those who wish to understand the reason of this steady recurrence of mystic tradition in every century, these studies may be of some use. They will serve as literary landmarks to guide the seeker to those distant sources whence flow faint echoes of divine truths—the heritage of the divine human race; truths that bring dim memories to the soul which are its highest impulse, and give the clue that guides it to the inner "science of the soul"—the mystic quest of all the saints, and the hidden truth that all religions have tried to teach, and which only a few in each religion have ever realized.

Mystics, visionaries, dreamers of vain dreams have been the names which the scoffers have always thrown at those who counted the world as nought compared with the treasure of the unseen life, and who devoted their lives to this divine science, and tried to reach an understanding of its laws. And as we trace out the records of the past it will be clearly seen that the Theosophical development is but another link in a wondrous chain of mystic teaching which stretches far back into the night of time.

Such a claim must be proved and its pretensions shown to be accurate, but it is only by careful researches in the historical dust-bins of the middle-ages that these data can be disinterred, and the chain of evidence rendered complete. Then it becomes evident that Theosophy is that glorious wisdom-religion which includes in its scope all religions and all philosophies.

And as we piece together the fragments of these historical relics, they waken delicate memories of the divine dreamer Dionysius the Areopagite, hallowed echoes of John Scotus Erigena, and thus we come face to face with the holy secrets of tender mystical souls who sought the true meaning of life. We get strange glimpses of the intense devotion of the scholastic divines, and monks to whom the unseen life was an intense and vital reality. The thoughts of Averroes and the Arabian mystics emerge—they who brought much of the Eastern truth and who founded the great occult schools of the once glorious Toledo, whence flowed a stream of thought, which formed the very life and soul of the heresies—so-called—of the Middle Ages. Nor may we omit the lore of the Eastern and Syrian monasteries to whom the books of Dionysius had taken the wisdom of Plotinus. Nor can the troubadours be passed by, the singers of mystic songs, and carriers of occult knowledge.

Singers, scholars, saints, and martyrs, a goodly array of men and women, all seeking the soul, and the soul's true world. Looked at from without, such a view appears like a worn mosaic pavement, broken, defaced, with many gaps lacking to make a perfect picture, and yet as we search and piece the apparently broken fragments the design begins to unfold itself, and finally the picture may be traced in perfect outline. For at the back of all these varying streams of thought there may be found one centre whence all diverge, and that great fount was named in ancient India, Brahma-Vidyâ, the Theosophia of the Neo-Platonists.

This ancient Wisdom Religion is the " thread-soul " on which are strung all the various incarnations and encasements of the religious life, adapted to the changing conditions and developments of humanity in its growth from childhood to manhood.

Begotten by that spiritual Hierarchy in whose guardianship is the evolution of the human race, brought forth from them, they, the guardians of the mystic tradition, give to those children of men who are strong enough for the burden, a portion of the real teaching of the Divine Science* concerning God and man, and the wonderful relationship that exists between the two.

With the passing of time the old orders changed, old forms perished, and the divine Sun that shone on the ever-changing screen of time veiled itself in new hues, and gathered into new groupings the humanity of the Western races, and each century which rolled by evolved a new phase of the ancient mystic tradition.

In the olden days men fought for their faiths, for they identified the form with that divine Life which lies at the back of all forms, and the changing of an outward veil shook their belief in the Holy Spirit, which it did but shroud. They feared change and sought to crystallize the Spirit, and this fear of change gave rise to that tenacious hold on outward ceremonies which has wrought so much evil in all the religions of the world.

---

* This " Science of the Soul " is the fact against which the Roman Church waged such bitter war, and formed the basis for the attack upon the various sects such as the Albigenses, Patarini, and Vaudois, all remnants of Gnostic sects.

INTRODUCTION.

Religious parties, secret societies, sects of every description, such is the shifting panorama of the religious life of Europe during the last eighteen hundred years, and as we glance back from our present standpoint, it is difficult at times to discern the mystic traditions, so loud is the clamour of contending sects over their formal doctrines, the outward expressions of their inner faith.

A word may here be said to guard against one error that might arise with regard to the spiritual Hierarchy before mentioned, the guardians of the world's religions. It is from this great communion that the World-Saviours have from time to time come forth, and from this centre have sprung all the " Sons of God."

The inception of all religions is from them, but lesser men build up the body; like wise teachers, they do not force dogmas on a child humanity. We see ordinary mankind prolific in building moulds for their faiths, heaping dogma upon dogma; but in tracing back all the religions to their founders, it may be seen that at the beginning the outward observances were ever subordinated to the inner life, the forms and ceremonies in fact, were merely organized in order to turn the attention of man to the inner and spiritual aspect of life. This method of training receives its completest exposition in the ancient code of Manu, where the whole daily life of ancient India was directed, by its very organization, towards the religious aspect. In the West this ideal was revived under the monastic orders, but since it was chiefly done under the rigid doctrinal supervision of the Catholic Church, the ideal of the simple spiritual life was crushed.

For the building of form—even religious form—is materializing in its tendency, and thus we see that in all the centuries subsequent to the inception of Christianity, the tendency of every "reformation" has been to throw back, if possible, to the original standard erected by the Founder. On careful investigation, for instance, the Christ appears responsible only for certain high and pure ideals, insistence being made on a holy life leading to a divine goal. The doctrines and elaborations which were later introduced arose in every case from the followers, who brought in their more worldly aims, and transformed thereby the purity and simplicity of the early ideal into an ornate body,* with wordly passions and constant strivings for mundane power.

Hence we find at the end of the nineteenth century, on one side the Catholic Church, on the

---

* "The favour and success of the Paulicians in the eleventh and twelfth centuries must be imputed to the strong, though secret, discontent which armed the most pious Christians against the Church of Rome. Her avarice was oppressive, her despotism odious; less degenerate, perhaps, than the Greeks in the worship of saints and images, her innovations were more rapid and scandalous."—Gibbon (E.), *Decline amd Fall of the Roman Empire*, Vol. IX., chap. liv., p. 289. In Italy the descendants of the Manichæans were termed Cathari, sometimes Gazari, or "The Pure." A good account, with many references, is to be found in Fuesslins (Johann Conrad), *Neue und unpartheyische Kirchen und Ketzerhistorie der Mittlern Zeit*. Frankfurt u. Leipzig, 1770.

other the Protestant, and between the extremes of these doctrinal communities, a fluctuating, ever-increasing body of thinkers, formed by the mystics and idealists of both parties, who from century to century have been at variance with their "orthodox" brethren, seeking a higher truth, a purer ideal, than those offered by the dogmatists.

The doctrines hidden in the secret fraternities have been handed down in regular succession from first to last. We can see that the esoteric teachings in Egypt, in Persia, and in Greece, were kept from the ears of an illiterate multitude precisely because it was known that they could not, in their then uneducated and ignorant condition, understand the deeper truth of Nature and of God. Hence the secrecy with which these pearls of great price were guarded and handed on with slight modifications into the possession of those grand early Christians, the Gnostics, the so-called heretics; then straight from the Gnostic schools of Syria and Egypt to their successors the Manichæans, and from these through the Paulicians, Albigenses, Templars and other secret bodies—these occult traditions have been bequeathed to the mystic bodies of our own times. Persecuted by Protestants on one side and by Catholics on the other, the history of mysticism is the history of martyrdom.

It is sometimes said that modern Theosophy is of sporadic growth and can show no sure basis, no line of religious or spiritual ancestry. But very little research proves the contrary, proves indeed that in spite of the many forms—religious bodies, secret societies, occult groups, Protestant reforms, and Catholic heresies—there is distinct evidence that there are certain points on which all of the various orders meet in accord, and that when these points are brought together, there appear self-revealed the same underlying teachings which form the basis of the great Wisdom Religion, parent and children standing out in unmistakable relation. For as King truly remarks:

Hippolytus . . . . . was right in calling all these heresies nothing better than the old philosophies disguised under new names; his only error lay in not going back far enough to find their ultimate source.*

Let us turn to that great conception, the doctrine of reincarnation, sometimes less correctly termed metempsychosis or transmigration. This tenet is the basis of the old Wisdom Religion, or Brahma-Vidyâ, and can be distinctly traced in all those mystic societies which draw their spiritual life from Gnostic sources. As Lecky† says:

The doctrine of transmigration was emphatically repudiated by the Catholics; the human race was isolated by the scheme of redemption, more than ever from all other races,

and it was against this isolation that the mystics,

---

* King (C. W.), *The Gnostics and their Remains*, p. 13. London, 1887.

† Lecky (W. E., M.A.), *History of European Morals*, Vol. II. p. 167. Third Edition. London, 1877.

or so-called heretics, struggled; this ancient doctrine of the transmigration of the soul was one of the heretical opinions for which the Cathari* were persecuted by the Catholic Church. It was very freely taught by the Troubadours in their mystic poems; a monk in his attack on Troubadour heretics mentions this doctrine with much scoffing and ridicule. We owe a debt of thanks to many such opponents, for they often show us where traces of the "Secret Doctrine" are to be found. For instance, it is to the orthodox and pious Catholic, Eugène Aroux, that we owe a mass of most important and valuable information on the Troubadours and their religious mission; their connection with mystic bodies, and the esoteric interpretation of their poems. Information as to their tenets which is not divulged by the mystics themselves is often given to us by their opponents, whose dissertations provide us with much evidence.

Such research indeed reveals a new phase, for out of the dim obscurity which shrouds the early centuries, undoubted historic evidence can be found of a wide-spread occult fraternity, which under various names has introduced into many societies the hidden aspect of spiritual truths, striving to avert the

---

* Says Lea: "Transmigration provides for the future reward or punishment of deeds done in life." Lea (Henry Charles), *A History of the Inquisition of the Middle Ages*, Vol. I., p. 91, 98. Schmid (C.), *Histoire et Doctrine de la Secte des Cathares ou Albigeois*, Vol. II., p. 256. Paris, 1849. Says: "La Metempsycose enseignée par l'une des écoles Cathares se retrouve également dans le Manichéisme."

materializing tendency by turning the eyes of men to the inner instead of the outer life.

Three principal streams of religious thought can be distinctly traced as we struggle through the labyrinth of evidences, and these may not inappropriately be termed the Petrine, Pauline, and Johannine doctrines, the last being the fountain-head of all the later Christian mystical heresies. The Johannine doctrine caused great excitement in the fourteenth century, the details of which will be given when we come to that period. It must be borne in mind that the true occultism, the real mysticism, is essentially religious in its nature, and students of Theosophy must not be surprised to find that some of the historical religious sects* have had their foundation in occultism and Theosophy. Such for instance are the Albigenses and the Waldenses, the forerunners of the Wesleyans, the Quietists and Quakers. These appear side by side with the Rosicrucians, the Knights Templars, the Fratres Lucis and many other sects who hold the same religious tenets.

This view will necessarily arouse some criticism, for the standard orthodox works on all the sects and heresies studiously omit every reference to occultism, and in some cases the real tradition can scarcely be

---

* The principal secret societies take St. John as their patron saint as we shall see when dealing with the details of many of these bodies. Notably is this the case with many of the Masonic bodies. See the articles on "Johannesbrüder" and "Johanneschristen" in *Allgemeines Handbuch der Freimaurerei*, Zweite völlig umgearbeitete Auflage; ii. p. 68. Leipzig, 1865.

INTRODUCTION. 15

found, so carefully is every reference to it extirpated from ordinary history.

It is only by searching into the records themselves that the real evidences of such esoteric doctrine are discovered, and it is in truth somewhat startling to find so many, while the outside public is in total ignorance of the very existence of a mystic tradition or a secret doctrine, or a spiritual Hierarchy. On this point a well-known writer on mysticism says:

The publication of the life and times of Reuchlin, who exercised so marked an influence over Erasmus, Luther, Melancthon, and the chief spirits of his age will, I trust, afford a key to many passages of the German Reformation which have not yet been understood in this country. They will reveal many of the secret causes, the hidden springs, which were moving the external machinery of several ecclesiastical reforms, which were themselves valuable rather as symbols of a spiritual undercurrent than as actual institutions and establishments. *Felix qui potuit rerum cognoscere causas.* Fortunate is it for the student of truth when he can thus discover the causes of effects, when he is allowed to examine the origin of those changes and revolutions, which but for this intelligible process would look like monstrous and unaccountable abortions, obeying no law and owning no reason. Fortunate is he who is thus allowed to step behind the scenes of the world's drama and hear the plans proposed and the pros and cons of the councillors which give rise to lines of action.*

Truly one could almost think a Theosophist was

---

* *The Life and Times of John Reuchlin or Capnion*, by Francis Barham (editor of the Hebrew and English Bible. London, 1843), p. 17.

writing the paragraph just quoted. The whole of Reuchlin's period will, we hope, be dealt with in due course, and a digest of the mysticism of this period made.

As already said, the occult doctrines of the Gnostics were heirlooms and sacred traditions from a very distant past, and when the early Christian era dawned, the human race had long been plunged in the darkening and materializing tendencies of the Black Age.* Soon indeed, the Gnosis was rejected by the orthodox church, and the sacred and secret teachings of the great Master Jesus became materialized; they have, however, never been lost, and traces of them can be discerned from epoch to epoch.

Says Marras† in his interesting study:

When therefore we speak of the continuation of their doctrines during the Middle Ages, we mean only a secret transmission of certain opinions, either in a number of families whose inner doctrines did not correspond to their outward profession of faith, or in the midst of certain sects which had had relations with the Gnostics. . . . . The vitality of the Manichæans was wonderful; notwithstanding the severe persecution they endured in the heathen as well as the Christian Roman Empire, they survived both in the East and in the West, and often reappeared in the Middle Ages in different parts of Europe. Manichæism dared to do what Gnosticism had never ventured upon: it openly entered the lists against the Church in the fifth century,

---

* The Kali-Yuga of the Hindus.

† Marras (P.), *Secret Fraternities of the Middle Ages*, pp. 19-21. London, 1865.

INTRODUCTION.

but the civil authority came to aid the religious authority in repressing it. The Manichæans wherever they appeared were immediately attacked : they were condemned in Spain in the year 380, and at Trèves in 385, in their representatives the Priscillianists; the Empire seems determined to annihilate Manichæism*, as well as Gnosticism when suddenly the latter arose under a new form and under a new name—that of Paulicianism.

In order that our readers may follow this line of study more clearly, it will be well to group the evidences of each century together. We must bear in mind that many of these societies stretch back through several centuries, and are not limited to one date or confined to one period. The consequent overlapping makes one of the difficulties of following these evidences of the secret tradition. Sometimes a body will remain the same, changing only its name, but keeping the same tenets. This is markedly the case with the Albigenses, the Paulicians, the Waldenses, and many of the middle age bodies —the Rosicrucians and others. Then again, we find that the same terms are sometimes used for the highest spiritual sciences and at others debased by the usage of charlatans. Theurgy, alchemy, mysticism, occultism, theosophy, yoga, all these names have

---

* In his last years the Pope had leisure to turn his arms against the Manichæan heretics, who, starting from the mountains of Bulgaria, carried their pure but stern religion westwards in a constant stream which never lost touch with its fountain-head, and under the names of Paterini, Ketzer, and Albigenses, earned the execration of their contemporaries, and the respect of posterity. Browning (Oscar), *Guelphs and Ghibellines : a short History of Mediæval Italy from* 1250-1409, p. 10, 1893.

been alternately used to indicate the purest and highest ideal of development for man, and then adopted by those who sought in them but their own selfish ends. To discriminate between these extremes, to find the true and leave the false mysticism, is then the aim in view. It is perhaps simplest to begin with the present era and trace the way back through the darkness of the middle ages to the period when the Gnostic schools still preserved to a great extent the sacred Eastern traditions.* The details of that period must be left to hands more skilled to treat the subject.

Let us then take a survey of the last nine centuries of the Christian era, and in a series of sketches substantiate with historical facts the proposition here but briefly outlined: that the ancient Wisdom Religion, or Theosophia, has had throughout these periods its votaries, teachers, messengers and followers, that the Great Lodge has never been without its representatives, and in truth that the guidance of the spiritual

---

* One curious fact which makes a further identity between these bodies is given by H. C. Lea, in his *History of the Inquisition of the Middle Ages*, Vol. I., p. 92. London, 1888. "A further irrefragable evidence of the derivation of Catharism from Manichæism is furnished by the Sacred thread and garment which were worn by all the Perfect among the Cathari. This custom is too peculiar to have had an independent origin, and is manifestly the Mazdean *kosti* and *saddarah*, the sacred thread and shirt, the wearing of which was essential to all believers, and the use of which by both Zends and Brahmins shows that its origin is to be traced to the prehistoric period anterior to the separation of those branches of the Aryan family. Among the Cathari the wearer of the thread and vestment was what was known among the inquisitors as the *hæreticus indutus* or *vestitus*, initiated into all the mysteries of the heresy."

evolution of the world by this body of teachers can be discerned by those who search the records.

The wave of gross materialism which swept over the Western world is now but slowly rolling away. The deplorable scepticism of our own day is but the result, and the natural result, of the methods adopted by the Catholic and Protestant Churches in the struggles of the Middle Ages. It has already been pointed out as one of the basic teachings of Theosophy that part of the evolutionary progress is the breaking up of forms in order that the spiritual nature of man may find wider conditions. In both of these Churches the extremes of dogmatic limitation were reached, the result being an ever increasing irritation of the more highly educated people against dogmas which were contrary to reason, and forms of faith which degraded the God they were supposed to uphold. For the Protestants believed in the verbal inspiration of an inaccurately translated Bible, claiming that their God gave his fiat in books whose historical basis is now shown to be unreliable. All who refused the letter of the law and sought the spirit which lay behind were cast out. We have but to search the records of the Puritans and some other Protestant bodies to see how rigid were their dealings with those who rejected their narrow theological dogmas.*

---

* See the execution and trial of Servetus, 1553, Willis (R., M.D.) *Servetus and Calvin. A Study of an important Epoch in the early History of the Reformation*; p. 480. London, 1877.

The Catholic Church permitted no education, no freedom of religious thought, and, knowing the unstable basis on which she stood, the Dominicans in the early middle ages took up the very simple position of entirely forbidding the reading of the Bible, except in such scamped versions as were authorized; and all who did not obey were removed by the Church. Indeed, the bloodiest and blackest records that history can show us are the attacks of the Catholic Church on the mystics of all these centuries.

"We do condemn to perpetual infamy the Cathari, the Patarines, the Leonists, the Speronists, and the Arnoldists circumcised, and all other heretics of both sexes by what name soever they are called. . . . And in case any man by a presumptuous attempt, being instigated thereto by the enemy of mankind, shall in any way endeavour the infraction of them [*i.e.*, the laws against the heretics] let him be assured, that by so doing, he will incur the indignation of Almighty God, and of the blessed Apostles Peter and Paul!"

Thus thundered Pope Honorius III. in the fourteenth century.* To give one solitary instance out of the numerous condemnations that fluttered about the mystic path.

Indeed it is hardly credible, even with the records open before us, that such inhuman tortures as were

---

* *History of the Christian Church*, by the Rev. Henry Stebbing, A.M. (London, 1834), ii., 301.

INTRODUCTION. 21

perpetrated on some of the mystic sects enumerated could have been devised in the name of a Saviour of mercy and love. Such fiendish barbarity, however, brought its own karma, a rich reward of hatred, scepticism and unbelief. The education and knowledge that the Church discountenanced and withheld were reached by natural evolution; the priests who should have been the spiritual leaders were overthrown and cast down, and the result was that education fell into the hands of materialistic and rationalistic thinkers, and the spiritual aspect of life was crushed out.

During the dark days of the revolution in France, it was the mystics who most bitterly deplored the growing scepticism. The materialists were the enemies of mystics, occultists and religionists of every kind, Catholic and Protestant. The Catholic party tried to father the outbreak of the revolution on the mystics. The Abbé Barruel in his book on Jacobinism * has taken every pains to do this, as also have the Abbé Migne and many others. But the appalling corruption of the Catholic Church, conjoined with her insistence on the ignorance of the people, was one of the great factors in that terrible outbreak.

In a very interesting correspondence between the Baron Kirschberger de Liebesdorf and Louis Claude de St. Martin,† the situation is most clearly described,

---

* *Barruel: Mémoires pour servir à l'Histoire du Jacobinisme*, 4 vols. London, 1797.

† Le Philosophe Inconnu, the leader of the Martinists.

and the following important extract shows the insidious method of work adopted by the German materialistic school, the enemy alike of mystics and Churches.

The Baron writes:

"MORAT, *June*, 1795.

" . . . . Unbelief has actually formed a well-organized club; it is a great tree which overshadows a considerable portion of Germany, bearing very bad fruit, and pushing its roots even into Switzerland. The enemies of the Christian religion have their affiliations, their lookers-out, and a well-established correspondence; they have a provincial for each department, who directs the subaltern agents; they control the principal German newspapers; these newspapers are the favourite reading of the clergy who do not like to study; in them they puff the writings which air their views, and abuse all besides; if a writer ventures to rise against this despotism, he can hardly find a publisher who will take charge of his manuscript. This is what they can do in the literary way; but they have much more in their power than this. If there is a place vacant in the public instruction department . . . they have three or four candidates all ready, whom they get presented through different channels; . . . in this way is constituted the University of Göttingen. . . . Another grand means which they employ is that of . . . calumny. This is all the easier for them, that most of the Protestant ecclesiastics, are, unhappily, their zealous agents; and as this class has a thousand ways of mixing everywhere, they can at pleasure circulate reports which are sure to hit their mark, before one knows anything about it, or is able to defend oneself. This monstrous coalition has cost its chief, an old man of letters at Berlin and at the same time one of the most celebrated publishers of Germany, thirty years' labour.

He has edited the first journal of the country ever since 1765; his name is Frederick Nicolaï. This *Bibliothèque Germanique* has, by its agents, taken hold also of the spirit of the *Literary Gazette* of Jena, which is very well got up, and circulates wherever the German language is known. Besides this Nicolaï influences the *Berlin Journal*, and the *Museum*, two works of repute. Political organization and affiliated societies were established, when these journals had sufficiently disseminated their venom. Nothing can equal the constancy with which these people have followed their plan. They have moved slowly, but surely; and, at the present hour, their progress has been so enormous, and their influence become so frightful, that no effort can now avail against them; Providence alone can deliver us from this plague.

At first, the march of the Nicolaïtes was very circumspect; they associated the best heads of Germany in their *Bibliothèque Universelle*, their scientific articles were admirable, and the reviews of theological works occupied a considerable portion of every volume. These reviews were composed with so much wisdom that our professors in Switzerland recommended them in their public discourses to our young Churchmen. But they let in the poison [of materialism] a little at a time and very carefully.*

This organized conspiracy was the result of the methods adopted by the Catholic Church. Men demanded knowledge, sought knowledge, and attained knowledge, but only of the material side of life. Shocked by the barbaric superstitions and illogical dogmas insisted on by the Church, the revolt of reason threw men back into a dogmatism which

---

* *La Correspondance inédite de L. C. Saint-Martin et Kirchœrger, Baron de Liebistorf* (1792-1797). Paris, 1862; pp. 195, 196.

was scarcely less rigid than the one they had left. The study of history, the knowledge of science, all tended to show the superficiality of that basis on which the Catholic Church had reared herself, and the leaders of thought who led this revolt, the Encyclopædists in France and the Nicolaïtes in Germany, were the bitter fruit of Catholic karma. They banded themselves together, and it was this body of sceptics and their organized conspiracy for which the Abbé Barruel and others tried to make the mystics responsible. The Church blamed others for the results of her own work, and the poison of unbelief and deadly materialism was meantime being slowly spread in Europe by the Nicolaïtes.

They tried to crush out all belief in or investigations into the unseen life and its forces. Hence their bitter and criminal attacks upon the Comte de St. Germain, Cagliostro, Saint Martin, and also upon the various mystical secret societies and Freemasonry in general. Keeping this powerful and malignant organization* in view, we shall better understand the charges brought against the various mystics above mentioned. It is only in the course of research that it is possible to realize the vindictiveness and argus-eyed watchfulness with which these Nicolaïtes pursued mysticism and Freemasonry. Article after article, book upon book, was produced, one and all from the same source, each teeming with the same poisonous

---

* The Nicolaïtes.

intent, the destruction of mysticism and the crushing out of the spiritual life.

The eighteenth century is perhaps the most difficult in which to sift the true tradition from the spurious; mushroom-like, semi-mystical societies sprang up on all sides, claiming occult knowledge and mystic teaching; but when these claims are sifted for verification they lack the stamp of high morality and purity which is the ineffaceable mark of all that emanates from the Great Lodge; hence in selecting the societies and bodies which will be dealt with and studied in detail, only those have been chosen in which outer and inner investigation proves their unmistakable origin to be from a source whose ideals are pure and holy.

That there was definite connection between the various sects, societies, and heresies, is evident; they had moreover a common language of signs, by which they could make themselves known to each other. Says Rossetti, speaking of the fourteenth century:

There are some events in history, whether literary, or political, or ecclesiastical, which at first sight appear to us quite enigmatical; but when once aware of the existence of the marked language of the secret Anti-papal Sects (especially of the Society of the Templars, and the Patarini, or Albigenses, or Cathari, with whom the learned in Italy were then so strictly connected), we find them very intelligible and clear.*

---

* *Disquisitions on the Anti-papal Spirit which produced the Reformation*, by Gabriele Rossetti, Prof. of Italian Literature at King's College (London, 1834), ii. 156. He is here referring to a secret language, the existence of which was known to many writers.

So that Rossetti speaks in the same manner as Barham in the passage already cited about a secret force* permeating the outer society. Again he says:

Why were the Templars, who were members of the most illustrious families in Europe, sacrificed by hundreds in different countries? Why were the Patarini burned alive in almost every city? History tells us: they belonged to secret societies, and professed doctrines inimical to Rome. What those doctrines were is well known, as far as regards the Patarini.†

Rossetti then proceeds to mention the Albigenses as a sect emanating from the Templars, who themselves held Eastern doctrines, a fact not found in the ordinary standard dictionaries of heresies, for the connection between those religious bodies, the Templars, the Rosicrucians, and the Freemasons is entirely suppressed, yet the historical links are all to be found by the unprejudiced student.

The rough enumeration which now follows of the mystical societies and so-called heresies serves only as a guide to where the evidence can be found.

---

* Says Lea in speaking of Calabria: "The Heretics sought and obtained in 1497 from King Frederic the confirmation by the crown of agreements. . . . They were visited every two years by the travelling pastors or *barbes*, who came in pairs, an elder known as the *reggitore*, and a younger, the *coadiutore*, journeying with some pretence of occupation, finding in every city the secret band of believers whom it was their mission to comfort and keep steadfast in the faith. . . . . Everywhere they met friends acquainted with their secret passwords, and in spite of ecclesiastical vigilance there existed throughout Italy a subterranean network of heresy disguised under outward conformity."—Lea (H. C.), *History of the Inquisition of the Middle Ages;* II., pp. 268, 269. New York; 1888.

† *Op. cit.*, I. 148.

They are, moreover, selected from many other bodies simply because in their inception they fulfil the before-mentioned conditions of purity and morality combined with occult knowledge. Some few societies, or groups rather, have been omitted simply because they are so occult that very little outer historical evidence is forthcoming. Facts are known about them by a limited number of people; but they stand more as the inspirers of the bodies here enumerated than in their ranks. A few names of leading mystics are also given, so that students may be able to trace the groups to which they are related.

Eighteenth century: The Fratres Lucis, or The Knights of Light; The Rosicrucians; The Knights and Brothers Initiate of St. John the Evangelist from Asia, or the Asiatische Brüder; The Martinists; The Theosophical Society*; The Quietists; The Knights-Templars; Some Masonic Bodies.

Seventeenth century: The Rosicrucians; The Templars; The Asiatische Brüder; Academia di Secreti, at the home of John Baptista Porta; The Quietists, founded by Michael de Molinos; and the whole group of Spanish mystics.

Sixteenth century: The Rosicrucians became widely known; The Order of Christ, derived from the Templars; Cornelius Agrippa, of Nettesheim, in connection with a secret association; Saint Teresa;

---

* Founded in London, 1767, by Benedicte Chastamer, a mystic mason.

St. John of the Cross ; Philippe Paracelsus ; The Fire Philosophers ; Militia Crucifera Evangelica, under Simon Studion'; The Mysteries of the Hermetic Masters.

Fifteenth century: The Fratres Lucis at Florence, also the Platonic Academy; The Alchemical Society; Society of the Trowel ; The Templars ; The Bohemian Brothers, or Unitas Fratrum ; The Rosicrucians.

Fourteenth century : The Hesychasts, or the precursors of the Quietists; The Friends of God ; German Mysticism, led by Nicholas of Basle ; Johann Tauler ; Christian Rosencreutz ; The great Templar persecution ; The Fraticelli.

Thirteenth century: The Brotherhood of the Winkelers ; The Apostolikers ; The Beghards and the Beguinen ; The Brothers and Sisters of the Free Spirit ; The Lollards ; The Albigenses, crushed out by the Catholic Church ; The Troubadours.

Twelfth century: The Albigenses appear, probably derived from Manichæans, who settled in Albi ; The Knights Templars, publicly known ; The Cathari, widely spread in Italy ; The Hermetists.

Eleventh century : The Cathari and Patarini, condemned by the Roman Church, both derived from Manichæans ; The Paulicians with the same tradition, also persecuted ; The Knights of Rhodes and of Malta ; Scholastic Mystics.

Tenth century: Paulicians: Bogomiles; Euchites ; Manichæans.

INTRODUCTION.

From the Ninth century to the Third century the following organisations and sects appear: Manichæans; Euchites; Magistri Comacini;* Dionysian Artificers; Ophites; Nestorians; Eutychians.

In the Fourth century the central figure for all occult students is the great Iamblichus; the forerunner of the Rosicrucians; and in the Third century we find Manes, the widow's son, the link for all of those who believe in the great work done by the "Sons of the Widow" and the Magian Brotherhood.

The various sects and bodies here detailed should not, of course, be understood as belonging exclusively to the century under which they appear in the above classification. All that this list is intended to convey is that such sects were more markedly prominent during the century in which they are placed.

The possibility of dealing with mysticism and the real mystic societies consists in the fact that we are dealing with a certain definite teaching, its difficulty consists in the fact that the outward presentation is constantly changing according to the exigencies of

---

* Llorente (J. A.). *Hist. of the Inquisition.* London, 1826. Merzario (Giuseppe, Prof.); *I Maestri Comacìni*; Milano; 1893. This author says: "In this darkness which extended over all Italy, only one small lamp remained alight, making a bright spark in the vast Italian necropolis. It was from the *Magistri Comacini*. Their respective names are unknown, their individual works unspecialized, but the breath of their spirit might be felt all through those centuries, and their name collectively is legion. We may safely say that of all the works of art between 800 and 1000, the greater and better part are due to that brotherhood — always faithful and often secret — of the *Magistri Comacini.*"

the period. New teachers are sent to build new forms, for the tendency to crystallize and to petrify is the natural inclination of the human mind ; the emotional nature clings fondly to familiar conditions, but these belong to the "natural body" and we are following the evolution of the "spiritual body." Through forms and phases many and painful does the soul acquire experience. Hence all these many societies have been but the schools through which the souls have been passing, and wherein they have acquired knowledge.

Thus the study of mysticism in the Middle Ages places before us a landscape flickering with shadow and with light, and the people who travel across that tract are alternately in light and shade, and their experiences, bitter as well as sweet, belong to all pilgrims who are seeking truth in the perplexities of the changing phases of human life.

TOWARDS THE HIDDEN SOURCES OF MASONRY.

As researches into its history are pursued, it appears more and more probable that the Masonic movement, to state it generally, was a sort of broad, semi-mystic and largely moral movement, worked from certain unknown centres, and deriving its origin from some ancient and not generally known basis. That is to say, its basis was, and is, unknown to all of those who do not recognise a definitely spiritual guidance in the practical, mental, and moral developments which from time to time change the surface of society by the introduction of new factors into the evolving processes of which life consists. Researches into Masonic literature must be made in many languages and countries before this view can be firmly established for the general world, but to the student of Theosophy who is also a student of Masonry it becomes more and more apparent that the movement which is generally termed Masonic had its roots in that true mysticism which originated, as an ideal effort, from the spiritual Hierarchy which guides the evolution of the world; and that, however much the branches may be separated from the root-idea, there is nevertheless a mystic teaching in Masonry for those who will seek below the surface.

One such searcher into the origin of Masonry gives the following interesting and suggestive passage in his study on the discoveries respecting the obelisk made by Commander Gorringe, which tend to "prove that an institution similar to Freemasonry existed in Egypt," and the writer proceeds:

According to our reading of history, the *priesthoods* of Belus, or Baal in Assyria, of Osiris in Egypt, of Jehova in Palestine, of Jupiter in Greece and Rome, of Ahura-Mazda in Persia, of Brahma in India, and of Teutates in Britain, were *primitive secret societies*, who instructed and governed the primitive families and races. It little matters whether we call the members of those priesthoods *Belites, Pastophori, Levites, Curetes, Magi, Brahmins, or Druids;* they were connected by secret ties, and intercommunicated from the Indus to the Tiber, from the Nile to the Thames. Hence there ever has been, is, and ever will be Freemasonry on our planet. Masonry was ever more or less connected with priesthoods till about the thirteenth century of our era, when Masons declared themselves *Freimaurer* (Freemasons). Since about that period priesthoods have ever denounced and persecuted Freemasonry.*

---

* Weisse, M.D. (John A.), *Obelisk and Freemasonry*, p.p. 94, 95. New York; 1880.

HIDDEN SOURCES OF MASONRY.

The evidences of the basic mystic teaching can be largely traced by watching the eddies and undercurrents which constantly break the smooth stream of ordinary Masonry. Frequently do we find other and smaller bodies, whose mystic aim was more marked and whose occult tendencies were more decidedly definite, springing up within the larger organization. Some few members with deeper insight gather round themselves others with the same tendencies, and thus we find formations of smaller societies constantly taking place. It is the main features of some of these that we are now going to outline, and after we have briefly reviewed the sources from which some of the leading Masons draw their historical Masonic tradition, we can pass from the general outline to the smaller societies, and it will be seen that the same traditions reappear in them.

And in corroboration of the hypothesis just enunciated, the words of a well-known Mason may be quoted, who in summing up an admirable lecture which had just been delivered by a Brother Mason spoke as follows:

A thoughtful consideration of our principal ceremony irresistibly leads us to the doctrine that was typified by the *pastos* in the King's Chamber of the great Pyramid, and connects with the main characteristic of all the mysteries, which embodied the highest truths then known to the illuminated ones.

. . . The twelfth century witnessed an outbreak of mystic symbolism, perhaps unparalleled in our era, and gave us the religious legends of the Holy Grail, which point to an eastern origin; this period coincides with the greatest popularity of the Templars, whose fall is contemporaneous with the decadence noticed by the lecturer.

Without pressing the argument, I may suggest that some portion, at least, of our symbolism may have come through a Templar source, Romanist yet deeply tinged with Gnosticism; while at a later date the Lollards (supposed to be inheritors of Manichæism) and who were but one of the many religio-political societies with which Europe was honeycombed, possibly introduced or revived some of these teachings. . . . . One thing is certain, that satisfactory renderings of our symbols can only be obtained by a study of eastern mysticism: Kabalistic, Hermetic, Pythagorean and Gnostic.

Down the centuries we find enrolled the names of philosophic teachers who veiled their doctrines in figures similar to those in vogue among the Rosicrucians and still more recent students, and often identical with the signs we blazon on the walls of our Lodges and Chapters.*

Many Theosophical students will find such utterances of immense value, as showing the view held by a Masonic authority of such well-known repute as Mr. E. Macbean, I.G., with regard to some, at any rate, of the Eastern links with modern Masonry.† Mr. Gould, the lecturer, also made the following suggestive remarks:

---

* *Ars Quatuor Coronatorum.* Transactions of the Lodge Quatuor Coronati, No. 2076. III., Part i., p. 31. London; 1890.

† Another Masonic authority says:—"A little later, or about the year 200 A.D., the most noteworthy Gnostic sect was a Persian branch, the Manichees; it was divided into three classes—Auditors, Elect, and Perfect, and the sect was ruled by twelve Apostles, with a thirteenth as President. Manicheism was always a source of trouble to the Church, and St. Augustine between the years 374 and 383 A.D., was an "Auditor," but for some reason

HIDDEN SOURCES OF MASONRY.

With regard to the derivations of Masonry, there are, briefly, three possibilities.

It may have come down to us
  I. Through a strictly Masonic channel.
  II. Through the Rosicrucians.
  III. Through a variety of defunct societies, whose usages and customs have been appropriated, not inherited, by the Freemasons.

The views thus put forward by these two authorities coincide perfectly with those of many German and Italian mystic writers of the last century and those preceding it. We will, therefore, investigate the early traditions in order to trace the links which bind them together, and join the chain to the yet more remote spiritual centre hidden, though not lost, in the clouds of time, and in piecing together

---

could not obtain advancement, and so abandoned the system. The Rite had a Theosophical Gospel which taught that the basis of all religion was one. In 657 they had changed their name to Paulicians, and later Cathari (purified), Euchites, Bogomiles, and in more recent times still, Lollards. We could quote numberless authors of the early period of the Church to prove the origin of these sects from the Eastern Magi, but it is unnecessary and space forbids. In a few words, they were a secret speculative society with degrees, distinguished by signs, tokens and words like Freemasonry, and the Church of Rome from the 4th to the 19th century has hated them with the hatred of death, butchering and burning them by tens of thousands; for Christianity has shed more blood than any other faith. Yet the fathers often admit their great purity of life, but that was their sin against a corrupt priesthood and unpardonable. The Templars were Gnostics, on the evidence of the Papal trials in 1313, and Hugh, G.M. 1118, is said to have received initiation from Theocletus, Patriarch of St. John the Baptist and the Codex Nazareus." *The Kneph*, Vol. V., No. 4, 1885. "Records and Documents relating to Freemasonry as a speculative society," by John Yarker, P.M., P.M.M.K., P.Z., P.E.C., P.R.G.C., &c. Chapter IV.—"Secret Theosophical Societies." (Continued from page 41.)

the fragments of these esoteric links it is better to begin with the views of a well-known Italian Mason, for it is to the "Sons of the Widow" we must look for help in revivifying the ancient spiritual truths of a once esoteric Masonry. The writer from whom we quote believed profoundly in Masonry and writes of it as one who knows that it was a vehicle for conveying spiritual mysteries to the people: Thus he writes* of the early history of Masonry:

Three centuries had passed since the origin of Christianity when at this epoch of barbarism there arose in the same Persia whence so many teachings had gone forth, a philosopher who wished to lead back the confused spirit of men to the cult of the only true God. He was called Manes. Some of the uninstructed have regarded him as the first originator of our Order, and the creator of our doctrines.

Manes lived under the Persian King Sopares. He endeavoured to recall to life in their entire purity the mysteries and the religion of Zoroaster, uniting them with the pure compassionate teachings of Jesus Christ. The teachings of Manes were liberal, whereas superstition and

---

* The quotations are taken from the German edition of the work of Reghellini da Schio, *La Maçonnerie considérée comme le Résultat des Religions Égyptienne, Juive et Chrétienne.* Paris, 1883.

See also Eckert (Edward Emil), *Die Mysterien der Heidenkirche erhallen und fortgebildet im Bunde der alten und der neuen Kinder der Wittwe.* Schaffhausen, 1860. Chap. vi., p. 77. "Die Manichäer oder die Kinder der Wittwe in Abendlande als Johannes-Brüder-und Schwesternschaft."

In this chapter Eckert traces the connection of the Manichæans or the "Children of the Widow" to the Johannes-Brüder of the West, and links them also to the German Building Corporations and Societies.

Chap. vii., 307. In this chapter he links them by their signs and symbols to the Cologne Masonic body of 1535.

despotism governed Europe. It is easy to believe that those who professed demagogic principles and a religion free from all that was chimerical would be persecuted. Thus the Manichæans from about the fourth century were persecuted to the fullest by all the despots and by the Romish Priests. . . . The Holy Augustine, brought up in the mysteries of Zoroaster adapted to the holy teaching of Jesus, became his bitterest persecutor and the greatest enemy to the teaching of Manes which was known under the name of the religion of the Child of the Widow.

This hatred shown towards Manes by St. Augustine, and his zeal for the Christian Trinity doctrine, may have originated in the vexation which Augustine experienced at having been only admitted into the first degree of the mysteries of Manes. The Magi, who had recognized in him an ambitious and restless spirit, were thereby induced to refuse to him all advancement, and this in spite of his nine years study, which he made in order to be raised to the higher degree. This fact is sufficiently confirmed by Fleury, Baronius, and by Augustine himself in his confessions. After the death of Manes, twelve of his pupils went forth into all the parts of the earth and imparted his teachings and his mysteries to all people. They illumined as with a lightning-flash Asia, Africa, and Europe, as may be seen from Baronius, Fleury, Bayle, and others. . . . . We have already said that still in the lifetime of Manes, his pupil Herman had spread his teaching in Egypt, where the Coptic priests and other Christians mingled it with the mysteries adopted from the Jews. . . . . . . It was through these same Coptic priests and the Eastern Christians that both the mysteries of the Children of the Widow, and the cult of the great Architect came to us in consequence of apparently unforeseen events, and it will be seen that it was principally by means of the Crusades that they obtained a secure footing in the West. The mysteries maintained their existence under the name of the cult of the Great Architect of the Universe, a name that has its origin in the allegory of Hiram, which represented, in the mysteries, "the unknown God," the Eternal, and sole creator of all things and the Regenerator of all beings.

Thus does Reghellini da Schio write, as he traces the Masonic ancestry back to the pre-Christian period, and he continues:

Bossuet in his *Histoire des Variations*, IV., says that in the middle ages the Christian sects, and especially the Manichæans and Gnostics, had concealed themselves as much as possible in the Orthodox Church itself: the remainder of the Manichæans who had maintained themselves only too well in the east, crowded into the Latin Church. Montfaucon, VII., p. 271, says when he speaks of the religion of the Egyptians, that the heresy of the good and evil principles which had been upheld by Manichæans, had at various times brought forth in the Church great disorder, and he asserts that in the East . . . . these doctrines existed at the time of the Crusades, ... the long time that elapsed during the wars of the Crusaders gave them the opportunity of being admitted into all the mysteries of the Children of the Widow, the teachings of the Great Architect of the world, and of both principles . . . . the Crusaders who had been admitted to the mysteries of the Children of the Widow and initiated therein, imparted them, on their return home, to their pupils in Europe . . . . . during the sojourn of the Crusaders with the Mussulmans, all kinds of theological investigations were instituted. These led the Crusaders deeper into the faith in the Great Architect of the world. . . .

And again in another passage (p. 46) he adds:

In spite of the religious and political changes that followed upon the conquests of the Saracens in Asia, Africa, and Europe; in spite of the persecutions introduced by them, the doctrines as to the unity of God was able to maintain itself by means of the Mysteries in Palestine, Syria, and Egypt, more especially, however, in the neighbourhood of Thebes; for here the Christians and Coptic priests preserved, in the lap of their solitude, the teachings communicated to them by Hesman, the pupil of Manes, a teaching which later passed over into Europe.*

Passing on from these important and interesting indications to the more detailed aspect of our subject we find that at a later period many of the semi-Masonic bodies had "Unknown Heads," and more especially those whose aims were avowedly occult, this being the term which was applied in Germany, Austria and Hungary to those organizations that did not make public the sources from which their teachings were derived, nor say from whom their inspiration came. To find the origin of such secrecy we must turn back to the early history of the Masonic tradition and sketch briefly what is told us by a Mason of the early part of this century, when dealing with this historic secrecy. He tells us:

We find among all the priests of ancient peoples, and in order that none but really capable and worthy men should be associated with their offices and studies, they instituted forms of probation and examination upon which followed some kind of initiation. Now as the oldest writers ascribed such mysteries and initiations to the Egyptian Priests, it is very probable that they already existed before the downfall of that people, for we find traces of them in equally ancient

---

* "Acerrellos" Rössler (Karl) *Die Freimaurerei in ihrem Zusammenhange mit den Religionen der alter Aegypter, der Juden, und der Christen:* II., p. 11. Leipzig, 1836.

nations and perceive from the likeness of their fundamental principles and of the teaching and customs of their priests, that they must have had a common origin. Among the Chaldeans the Magi dwelt on the summits of the mountains, and among the Celtic races the Druids lived in the quiet solitude of the forests. Among the Indians and Ethiopians the Brahmins and Gymnosophists had localities specially dedicated to them, and among the Egyptians the Priests had intricate dwelling-places far beneath the surface of the earth. All had their symbols and distinctive signs, and owed their fame only to the secrecy of their initiation.

The secrets of Antiquity had a twofold aim. In the first case religion was chosen as the object of care; the greater the mysteries the more eternally secret were they to be kept from the people. The aim in the second case was to guard the Wisdom of all things. He who would be initiated must be a man of upright character and true mental power. The sacred mysteries fell into decay with the Roman Empire, the flourishing and spread of the Christian religion being the chief cause of this decadence. The initiation into the mysteries of the Wisdom was however of much longer duration. They changed only from time to time either the name, the inner constitution, the degrees and various kinds of knowledge bound up in these, or even the nature of the union itself. The men, who were known under the name of Magi, or the White Masters, made one of their most important aims the true knowledge of the human heart, which lay always open before their eyes. To them alone was entrusted the bringing up of Kings and the great of the earth, for they alone could understand science as well as art, and careless of all prejudice taught a simple and natural theology, which based itself upon the worship of a Supreme Being.

Because, however, their method of teaching was symbolical, many errors of which they were entirely incapable were ascribed to them on account of their numerous hieroglyphics. The Magi of Memphis and Heliopolis were held in such esteem, and their renown was so widespread that the greatest heroes of war, philosophers, and strangers of the highest rank journeyed to Egypt and sought to be initiated by the Priests in order to learn the secrets of the Priesthood. From among these priests Lycurgus and Solon drew a part of their system of philosophy; and Orpheus was also initiated by them, and by this means enabled to introduce into his own land, festivals from which the Greek mythology afterwards arose. Thales also was instructed by them, Pythagoras received from the same source his doctrine of Metempsychosis, Herodotus obtained much information, and Democritus his secrets. Moses also, who was brought up by the Magi, used his knowledge of the mysteries to free the Israelites from Egyptian bondage and lead them to the service of the true God. It is well known that Moses prescribed certain probation for his Levites, and that the secrets of the Priesthood were inaccessible to the rest of the Israelites, and this principle ruled till the time of Solomon.*

And this policy of silence was a wise one, for the bitter vituperations which were showered on the heads of the few who were the exoteric leaders in such organizations, demonstrated the wisdom which guarded the personalities of the real leaders. Such

---

* *Sarsena, oder der Volkommene Baumeister, enthaltend die Geschichte und Entstehung des Frei-Maurerordens.* Bamberg, 1816. The author of this work is not definitely known, but another Mason, Herr Z. Funck, wrote, in 1838, the *Kurze Geschichte des Buchs Sarsena*, Bamberg, and said of the above work: "There are few books which on their publication caused so great a sensation as did this one. . . . the author of this work was an old experienced Freemason." The publisher says that 1500 copies were sold in the first month, and it went through five editions; it caused, moreover, a miniature Masonic warfare. Written by one who knew what Freemasonry should be, it naturally raised the violent opposition of those who wished to drag it away from its mystical standpoint.

work was better done by small groups, and this appears to have been the view held by those leaders with whom the student does come into contact. Some few of these groups in the last century have already been cited,* but it will be as well to repeat their titles, which run as follows :

The Canons of the Holy Sepulchre.

The Canons of the Holy Temple of Jerusalem.

The Beneficent Knights of the Holy City (The Strict Observance).

The Clergy of Nicosia in the Island of Cyprus.

The Clergy of Auvergne.

The Knights of Providence (The Order of the Knights of St. Joachim).

The African Brothers.

The Knights of Light (The Order of Fratres Lucis).

The Asiatic Brothers (The Order of the Knights of St. John of Asia).

These Societies do not belong to any one country in particular, for we find ramifications of them appearing, disappearing and re-appearing, like beacon lights, in Austria, Hungary, Italy, France, Sweden, and Russia. England was the least prolific soil in the early centuries for the implanting of this mystic seed. In Scotland and Ireland, however, that light shone more clearly than in England. But in Austria and the Danubian Provinces mysticism grew apace for a short and happy while, and so a few words about Austria in particular may be said before passing on.

---

* *The Theosophical Review*, xxii. 311.

HIDDEN SOURCES OF MASONRY.

Says Ludwig Abafi, in his *Introduction to Pre-Historic Freemasonry in Austria and Hungary*:*

It is proved that the Emperor Rudolph I., even in the year 1275, authorized an Order of Masons, whilst Pope Nicholas III., in the year 1278, granted to the Brotherhood of Stonemasons at Strassburg, a letter of Indulgence which was renewed by all his successors down to Benedict XII. in 1340. The oldest order of German Masons arises in the year 1397; next follow the so-called Vienna Witnesses of 1412, 1430, and 1435; then the Strassburg Order of Lodges of 1495; that of Torgau of 1462, and finally sixteen different Orders on to 1500, and to the following centuries for Spires, Regensburg, Saxon-Altenburg, Strassburg, Vienna, and the Tyrol.

At this period the Roman Church appears to have made various futile efforts to retain a hold upon these Masons, but without tangible result. For the forces at the back of these movements prevented the destruction of a new free spiritual growth by the Roman power. At this period also came those great souls, burning for freedom, who worked the Reformation,† and although that work and those reforms were

---

* *Geschichte der Freimaurerei in Oesterreich und Ungarn.* Buda-Pest, 1890-1891. Pt. I., p. 8.

† Such, for instance, as John Tauler, the famous Dominican (born 1290, died 1361), who formed a mystical fraternity, the members of which recognized each other by secret signs. Then we have Nicholas of Basle, with his four disciples, the beginning of the "Friends of God." These men kept a watch on all that was going on in the world, and they had special messengers who had certain secret signs, by which they recognized each other; Nicholas was burned as a heretic. Much information concerning this sect is given in a MS. called *The Book of the Five Men.* (1377). See for details, Jundt (A.), *Les Amis de Dieu au XIVme Siécle.* Paris 1879.

dwarfed of their full growth by the natural crudity and narrowness of the human mind, nevertheless the dogmatic and mind-killing power of Rome was materially thwarted, and the spirit in the teaching of the Master Christ set free from those trammels. At all events, Abafi proceeds:

> Equally important in the formation of Freemasonry . . . . were certain religious communities and brotherhoods of the Middle Ages, which for the most part aimed at a return to the pure teaching of Christ, and at making its ethical form familiar to their adherents. One of these brotherhoods was that of the Waldenses, established by Peter Waldo in the year 1170 at Lyons. Their aim was the restitution of the original purity of the Church through the adoption of voluntary poverty, and other ascetic practices. But because of the doctrine of Transubstantiation they soon came into conflict with the Catholic Church, and as early as 1134 Pope Lucius III. excommunicated them, and Sextus IV. in 1477 proclaimed a Crusade against them. In spite of these attacks they have kept alive up to the present day, and have spread into several countries, namely into Italy, France and Bohemia, and in this latter country we shall meet them again under the name "Bohemian Brothers."

A few words may be summarised from the same writer about some of the other mystic bodies in Bohemia and Hungary, lands full of occult tendencies. Among them are the following: "Die Brüder von Reif und Hammer," or the "Brothers of the Circle and Hammer," "Die Hackebrüdershaft," "The Brotherhood of the Hatchet," "Die Freunde vom Kreuz," or the "Friends of the Cross." This last society spread into the Netherlands, and had its greatest success in the latter part of the 17th Century. The "Brothers of the Cross"* were still holding their meetings in 1785: they had many members in Wallachia, and still more in Transylvania.† Brabbée in his Masonic studies says: It consisted principally of

Older men and those who were generally reputed wise, and therefore of the prominent leaders of the Brotherhood, who here, in the Metropolis of the Kingdom, formed a kind of stronghold of the "inner East."

The last expression is worthy of our notice, for it shows how the minds of men were turning, even in Masonic circles, to the Eastern teachings. Abafi also says that a great and moulding force was exercised at this period on the form of Freemasonry by Jan Amos Komensky (latinized Comenius) who was born at Brünn, in Bohemia, in 1592, and who became a chaplain of the Bohemian Brothers in 1618. When the civil wars began Komensky lost wife, child, and property, and was exiled from Austria like all other non-Catholics. He escaped to Poland, turned his thoughts to educational matters, and became famous in Sweden, Hungary, and England.

Komensky was actively interested in the Rosicrucian movement, and joined John Valentinus Andreas in his work in that body. In 1650 Komensky was

---

* Sometimes called Fratres de Cruce.
† Brabbée (Gustav), *Sub-Rosa Vertrauliche Mittheilungen aus dem Maurerischen Leben unserer Grossväter*, p. 25. Wien, 1879.

invited to Hungary and Transylvania by the Prince Ragozcy, where he stayed four years. It is doubtless partly owing to his influence that the Rosicrucian movement spread so widely in these countries. His philosophical and metaphysical views were so widely spread, that when Anderson* wrote his book on Freemasonry, he, according to Abafi, incorporated in his work a compilation of the most essential portions of the plans of Komensky. As Abafi phrases it :

It was reserved for an Austrian, a Moravian schoolmaster, the Chaplain of the Bohemian Brothers, to bestow ethical treasures upon a brotherhood in proud Albion, the home of the boldest intellects ; to formulate the ideas, and to point out the way for a league which—after its transformation—was destined to embrace the noblest of all nations, and being brought to perfection by them, ordained to influence the whole of humanity.

The spread of mysticism in Austria and Hungary during the last century was astoundingly rapid ; according to one authority† about five per cent. of the entire population belonged to the Freemasons, Rosicrucians, and other allied societies.

The vast majority of these Lodges must, he thinks, have been secret, for at the death of the

---

* James Anderson, D.D,, whose work was published in 1723, under the title *The Constitutions of the Freemasons ; containing the History, Charges, Regulations, etc., of that Most Ancient and Right Worshipful Fraternity, for the use of the Lodges.* A second edition, revised, was published in 1738.

† *Freimaurer;* Heft. I., p. 10, ed. by von Andrée. Gotha, 1789.

Empress* only three legitimate and perfect Lodges existed. That is to say, only three Lodges in which Freemasonry as such existed without any more extended search into occultism. Another authority, Dr. Otto Henne-am-Rhyn,† promptly doubles this number, saying that there were 20,000 mystic students in Vienna. As this writer was an avowed enemy of mysticism, his views may be taken as not likely to exaggerate the numerical value of occult students.

In Austria mysticism had been aided by the kindly interest taken in such subjects by the Emperor Francis I. He had protected and favoured a very remarkable man called Seefels—or Sehfeld—a Rosicrucian and Mason, who had an alchemical laboratory at Rodaun, a small village about a mile from Vienna. This man was loved and respected by the whole neighbourhood for his kindliness, as well as feared for his powers, which were most remarkable. Seefels is mentioned by Schmieder in his valuable History of Alchemy,‡ as one of the "Seven true Adepts" who should appear in Europe in the course of the century. Schmieder also gives some very interesting proofs of his powers. But in spite of the Emperor's protection he was seized by

---

* Maria Theresa, wife of Franz I., and the mother of Joseph II. of Austria.

† Henne-am-Rhyn (Otto), *Kulturgeschichte des Zeitalters der Aufklärung*, v., p. 244. Leipzig, 1878.

‡ Schmieder (C. C.), *Geschichte der Alchemie*, pp. 527-542, 1832.

the police and placed in the fortress at Temeswar in Hungary. A careful study of Schmieder's work would more than repay any student who desires to have evidences for occult powers made certain by history.

The following interesting notes* are quoted as showing the connecting link between the Continental mystic Masonry and England, of which but little has been heard in the outer world.

In a German tract, printed about 1803, and bound up with another tract of Fessler's, called *Geschichte der Freimaurerei*, occur the following startling statements, which I give to Masonic students for what they are worth.

1. The Templars worked with the so-called "Magical Brethren" at an early period of their existence.

2. A Rosicrucian MS. states that at Cologne, with the motto, "*non omnis moriar*," this Magical Union was created there in 1115.

3. A MS. of Michael Mayer's still exists in the University Library at Leyden, which sets forth that in 1570 the Society of the old Magical Brethren, or "Wise Men" was revived under the name of Brethren of the Golden Rosy Cross.

4. It is asserted that in 1563 the statutes of the Brotherhood were, on the 22nd of September, at Basle, at a meeting of seventy-two Masters of Lodges, revised, set forth, and printed; that the Lodges of Swabia, Hesse, Bavaria, Franconia, Saxony, Thuringia, and those on the Moselle acknowledged the headship of the Grand Lodge of Strassburg. That in the eighteenth century the Lodges of Dresden and Nuremberg were fined by the Grand-Master of Strassburg, and that the Grand Lodge of Vienna, of Hungary,

---

* See *The Kneph*, vol. iv., 3. August, 1884. "Masonic Notes."

HIDDEN SOURCES OF MASONRY.

and Stirrmark, the Grand Lodge of Zürich, which ruled the Swiss Lodges, referred to the Mother Lodge of Strassburg in all difficult and doubtful matters.

To these notes by a "Masonic Student" the following editorial note is appended:

There can be no doubt that the Theosophical and Magical Union above mentioned did exist as an organized Secret Society. The correspondence of Cornelius Agrippa von Nettesheim shows that he was a member of such a secret society, and it is further asserted that when he was in London he established a branch of it in that city. Fludd, as showing that secret societies existed in the Universities, has the passage "notwithstanding any allegiance which I may have vowed by a ceremonial Rite to Aristotle* in my youth." These societies used the double Triangles, or Seal of Solomon, and in the ruins of one of the old Temple Preceptories in France was found a copper medallion with the Lamb surmounted by this Cabalistic symbol.

Two points in this interesting note can be corroborated by further evidence. The Rosicrucian MS. mentioned in para. 2, is also mentioned on page 56 of a most valuable German book (to which reference has already been made) by Friedrich Gottlieb Ephraim Weisse, or Magister Pianco; it is called *Der Rosenkreutzer in seiner Blösse* (Amsterdam; 1781). Some extracts from it will not be without interest, for it refers to the older body of "Wise-Men," who were known as the "Unknown Heads" of many of the

---

* Says Accelleros (Dr. Karl Rössler): "The Gnostic principles were spread under the form of Aristotelean Philosophy at Paris and elsewhere."—*Die Freimaurerei in ihrem Zusammenhange mit den Religionen der alten Aegypter, der Juden und der Christen*, II., p. 63. Leipzig, 1836.

small societies. The conditions of entrance are briefly given as follows:

3. Whosoever wished to be admitted to the secrets, and afterwards to be initiated, must be a man of honour and of true spiritual power; and he must be already of considerable learning; for only those were accepted, of whom it could be hoped that they would be of great service to the Sacred Alliance. . .

10. The Initiates wore a triangle, symbolical of the three qualities of the Demiurgos—Power, Wisdom and Love. . . .

The Masters of the second secret were Masters in the knowledge of all nature, and her forces, and divisions.

11. They were called Philosophers or the World-Wise. Their science was called the World-Wisdom. . . .

12. These World-Wise occupied themselves in secret. No one knew where they met, or what they did.

14. But they had also secret sciences known only to the highest among them—called Magos, Mage, or the Wise Master, who taught the people of Divine things. He could do things which appeared quite supernatural. *

The author, speaking of the relation of Masonry to this older and more secret body, says:

Those Brother Masons (of the highest degrees) knew that they owed their brotherhood to the Initiations of the old Wise-Men; that the great part of their (the Masons') knowledge came from Them, and that without Their help they could do nothing. †

In another passage he says:

Long before the year 1118, there was a society which in the mysteries of the ancients took the place of the last and

---

* *Op. cit.*, pp. 28, 30-32.   † *Op. cit.*, p. 54.

youngest grade, and which had the same position with the Tempelherren, who had adopted it with the other teachings of the Wise Ones.—They were the novices from all time. As in the time of the Inquisition against the Templars no one knew anything about the lower and last grades, and those who belonged to them had no public connection with them and thus lived without attracting any attention, they were overlooked in the cruelties of the time. One did not think of them. As the members of the Templars who escaped were few in number and died one after the other, the remaining members drew together to form a bond of friendship, to which end they drew up certain rules. This new society appeared in different forms and under different names, Cross Society or Brothers of the Cross, Noaites, and in later days adopted the name of Freemasons.

Length of time and the involved issues consequent thereon made those initiated into the Mysteries at length perceive that they must introduce an entirely different organization into the community, in order to bring it into line with Christianity.

Those associates who still remained over from the collapse* of the community of Initiates, and who were scattered about the world, began to make fresh projects for a general union. They took the laws of their community and the laws of the Christians, which are known under the name of the Bible, into a real assimilation. They began to institute a parallel between the books of Moses and the memorials of the Magi, and from all this they evolved a kind of association, provided with certain laws, which could fit in with the Christian.

The association was, as is always the custom with innovations, in the beginning somewhat dark and involved; it was saddled with various meanings and names, which it

---

* The writer is referring to the persecutions of the "Magian Brothers," who followed Manes the reformer.

would be quite unnecessary to repeat here, but which were all of short duration, so that the first ones called it the association of Magi and its members the Magi Brotherhood and associates. And this first association was formed in the year 1115 and lasted till the year 1117, though it underwent changes from time to time. The Crusaders had given rise to many societies and orders amongst the profane, and associations had sprung up which had quite differing objects. Amid innumerable ones there arose in the year 418 the Knights, with whom the Magi Brotherhood united and shared their principles and secrets with them.

The writer speaks "as one having authority" and knowledge also.

Turning to the particular date mentioned in the notes from *The Kneph*, we find that about this period, or a few years earlier, the first documentary evidence of the appearance of the Asiatische Brüder is mentioned by the Baron Hans Ecker von Eckhoffen in his treatise, *Authentischen Nachrichten von den Ritter- und Brüder-Eingeweihten aus Asien* (Hamburg; 1788). These writings, he says, date from 1510; showing that a body of mystics was known at that period; these Knights of Asia also called themselves the Knights of St. John, and it is a curious fact to notice that one of the Masonic records which has caused an infinity of discussion, and also of dissension, amongst Masons, is the celebrated "Cologne Record" which is dated 1535, and in which an Order of St. John is noticed. This charter has been a veritable bone of contention between materialistic and mystic Masons, and much polemical literature

HIDDEN SOURCES OF MASONRY.

has been published on the subject. The mystics hold it to be true on external and internal evidences; while the materialists reject it, as they reject all such evidence.

In the record there is the name of Philip Melancthon—the friend and co-worker of Martin Luther—who appears as a Brother in the Order of the Freemasons. This document bears witness also that a secret society was known in various parts of the world, which existed before 1440 under the name of the "Brotherhood of St. John," and since then, and up to 1535, under the title, the "St. John's Order of Freemasonry" or "Masonic Brotherhood."

This Society* was reformed and re-arranged in the year 1717, the generally accepted modern date of the materialistic and non-mystic Masons. It became more atheistic in its views, and more democratic in its tendencies. Amongst other deeply interesting matter, the "Charter of Cologne" contains the following passage:

> The Brotherhood, or the order of Freemason Brothers, bound together according to St. John's holy rules, traces its origin neither from the Templars nor from any other spiritual or temporal Knightly Order, but it is older than all similar Orders, and has existed in Palestine and Greece, as well as in various parts of the Roman Empire. Before the Crusades our Brotherhood arose; at a time when in consequence of the strife between the sects teaching Christian morals, a small number of the initiated—entrusted with the true

---

* The present Freemason body.

teaching of virtue, and the sensible exposition of the secret teaching—separated themselves from the mass.*

According to the record, the following reason was given for the adoption of the name : The Masters of this confederation were called the St. John's Brethren, as they had chosen John the Baptist, the forerunner of the Light of the World . . . as their original and example.†

There is a curious similarity between this document in its phrasing and style, and the remarks made in the book by Weisse, in his *Der Rosenkreutzer in seiner Blösse*, some passages of which have already been summarised.

Yet another well-known Masonic authority bears witness to the value of the Cologne Record. Thus Mackenzie writes :

The documents are still preserved in one of the Lodges at Namur. They have been very hotly debated. On the one hand, Oliver, Reghellini, and some others treat them as authentic, and the antiquaries of the University of Leyden certify that the paper on which the register of the Lodge at the Hague is written is of the same kind as that used in Holland in the beginning of the seventeenth century. Now this register refers to the Charter of Cologne as being in existence, so that the fraud, if a fraud, is two centuries old.‡

Our chief interest in all this detailed evidence lies in the ever-recurring testimony that it bears to that older Fraternity, which was the inspiring body at the

---

* *Freimaurer Lexicon*, Gädicke (J. C.). Berlin ; 1818.

† J. G. Findel's *History of Freemasonry*, p. 721. Translated from 2nd German ed. with preface by G. von Dalen. London ; 1866.

‡ *The Royal Masonic Cyclopædia*, p. 126. London ; 1877.

back. But we must now turn to some of the societies which had "Unknown Heads," as given in our list.

J. M. Ragon, in his *Orthodoxie Maçonnique*, gives the following interesting account of one of these bodies, more information on which will be added from other sources.

Order of the Architects of Africa, or the African Brothers (*1767*).

This Order was composed of educated and well-principled brothers. Their lodges, in Europe, were all closed, excepting perhaps that of Constantinople (at Berlin).

Only one of their Grand-Masters was known; this was the councillor of war, Köppen.

Their first degree offered a more extensive and complete instruction than all the degrees of the Scotch systems together. They said that the Lodges of St. John neglected the great end, and that instruction was hardly to be had there, and that the Strict Observance did not know the grounds of the continuation of the Masonic Order. They occupied themselves with hieroglyphics, especially with those relating to Freemasonry, which they sought to know well. They made a mystery of their goal up to the seventh degree, which could only be gained by zeal, perseverance and discretion. Their secondary occupations were the sciences, especially history and antiquities, the study of which they considered indispensable for the true Freemason.

Their first degree was symbolically called the Architect or Apprentice of Egyptian secrets.

They called themselves the Africans,* because their

---

* This tradition came from Egypt and passing along North Africa, swept over into Spain, and was at the foundation of the great Arabic mystic development which has made Spain immortal. The true name

studies began with the history of the Egyptians, in whose mysteries they found indications of Freemasonry, although they placed its origin much later, as to which the Crusades gave them no light.

Their customs were simple and noble. They never laid any stress on decorations, aprons, ribbons, jewels, etc., but they liked a certain luxury, and sententious inscriptions with a sublime but hidden meaning. In their assemblies they read treatises and communicated to each other the result of their researches.

Their banquets were simple, decorum prevailed, and instructive and scientific discourses were given at them.

Admissions were given without any fees. Earnest brothers who fell into distress received much assistance.

They have published many important documents in Germany on Freemasonry.

This Order was established in Prussia, in 1767, with the assent of Frederick II., called the Great.

Its degrees, to the number of eleven, were divided into two temples, viz.:

First Temple.
    1. Apprentice.
    2. Companion.
    3. Master.

Second Temple.
    4. Architect, or Apprentice of the Egyptian secrets (Manes Musæ).
    5. Initiate in the Egyptian secrets.
    6. Cosmopolitan Brother.
    7. Christian Philosopher (Bossinius).
    8. Master of the Egyptian secrets, Aléthophilote (Friend of Truth).

---

of this African tradition is Manichæism, and in the Church of North Africa the Gnostic teaching lived for many a century: and among the Copts the tradition yet endures.

Higher Degrees.
  9. Armiger.
  10. Miles.
  11. Eques.

The Grand Chapter gave each year, during the life of Frederick II., a gold medal of 50 ducats as a prize for the best treatise or discourse.

In 1806 only one Chapter of this system remained, that of Berlin ('Constantinople').

On the supposed origin of the Order, Ragon writes as follows:

When Frederick II. came to the throne, seeing that Freemasonry was no longer what it had been, and appreciating what it might be, he conceived the plan of an Inner Order which might at the same time take the place of a Masonic Academy. He made choice of a certain number of Masons capable of comprehending his ideas, and charged them with the organization of this body. Among these were to be noticed the brothers Stahl, de Gone, Meyerotto and du Bosc. They instituted the Order under the name of an extinct society, The Architects of Africa, and established statutes in accordance with the views of the King, who on his side granted privileges, and in 1768 had erected in Silesia, by his architect Meil, a building specially designed for the Grand Chapter, and endowed it with an ample fund, with a choice library and rich furniture, the whole being of an elegance worthy of the Order and of the King.

This Order, without pretending to dominion, teaching tolerance, professing the primitive principles of Freemasonry, and making a special study of its history, prospered in silence and in complete freedom. Its chief statutes were to fear God only, to honour the King and to be discreet, to exercise universal tolerance towards all Masonic sects without ever affiliating itself to any. It was for this reason that they never submitted to the act of obedience of the Baron de Hund, notwithstanding all the entreaties that were made to them to do so. In the admission of candidates they observed the strictest caution. It is said that Duke Ferdinand of Brunswick was refused because he meddled with sectarian affairs. They devoted themselves to active researches into the history of the mysteries, of secret societies and their various branches, and cultivated the sciences, chiefly mathematics. In their works, carried on often in Latin, reigned morality, a high tone, a solid and unostentatious teaching.

Their library and their archives obtained through the protection of the King and of persons of distinction, among others the Prince von Lichtenstein at Vienna, some real treasures of manuscripts and documents, which no Masonic branch can boast. (*Découverte sur le Systéme de l'Ordre des Architectes Africains, Constantinople.* Berlin; in 8vo, 51 pp., 1806.) This article is taken from the Masonic library of the very kind brother, Th. Juge.*

Few monarchs have more thoroughly protected the Mystic Schools within the Masonic body than Frederick II., King of Prussia, well named "The Great." Not only did he protect them, but he also actively sympathised with them. While still Crown Prince, he was initiated as a Mason at Brunswick in August, 1738, and was from that period the staunch protector of the Masonic Fraternity; nor did he omit to penetrate very deeply into the early traditions of Masonry, far more so, indeed, than many who have fewer duties to engage their time.

Frederick the Great was, however, by no means the

---

* Ragon, op. cit., pp. 239, *et seq.*

vague and dreamy mystic of popular representation; his academy and schools were the centres of the most brilliant intellects of the period, while the choice of his friends, literary, philosophical, and mystic, testifies to the breadth of his knowledge, and it also illustrates the manifold sympathies of his nature, both as soldier and mystic, philosopher and scholar; though not saintly, by any means, he was thoroughly appreciative of ideals that were beyond him.

His sympathy with mystics is evidenced by his selection of a librarian, for he gave that post at the Royal Public Library in Berlin, with the title of Academician, to Dom Antoine Joseph Pernetty (or Pernety), a man who had been a Benedictine monk,* but having become—like many others—dissatisfied with the Order, he applied to the Pope for a dispensation from his vows. This was no obstacle in the eyes of the King, deeply interested as he was in the researches of this well-known Hermetist and Alchemist.

That the opinions of Dom Pernety were publicly known is demonstrated by a writer of the period, who says:

A remarkable trait in the character of this Academician was, that he believed in the philosopher's stone,

---

* Benedictine Monk of the Congregation of Saint-Maur, Abbot of Burgel in Thuringia, Librarian of the King of Prussia: author of *Les Fables égyptiennes et grēcques devoileés et réduites au même Principe*, *Le Dictionnaire Mytho-Hermétique*, and other treatises on Alchemy.

the mysteries of the Cabala, apparitions, patagonians, witcheries, enchantments, the race of giants, etc. But, notwithstanding this inconceivable and ridiculous weakness, he was beloved by everyone, and the more as, to his other excellent qualities, he joined that of the most perfect discretion in regard to such affairs as were at any time confided to his secrecy; never did a word from his lips give room for the smallest explanation or disagreement.*

Such is the comment on this mystic's character by one who, while adverse to his opinions, nevertheless renders justice to a personality which some traduced.

Dom Pernety was for some time in personal relationship with M. de St. Germain; and later on, he founded the Académie des Illuminés d'Avignon, which was essentially Hermetic in its aims, and had also a close connection with the Swedish system. This was a secret body, but it was also under the general Masonic regulations. It was also in close union with the followers of Martinez Pasquales, and that bond has been kept up, for some of the treatises written by Dom Pernety are now being published by the Martinists in America. To pursue this interesting topic would, however, lead us too far from our "Afrikanische Bauherren" and their protector, the King of Prussia, with whom our attention is at present engaged.

The most succinct account of the opinions held by

---

* *Original Anecdotes of Frederic II., King of Prussia*, translated from the French of Dieudonné Thiébault, Professor of Belles-Lettres in the Royal Academy of Berlin, II., p. 383. London, 1805.

HIDDEN SOURCES OF MASONRY. 61

the leading Freemasons in Germany at this juncture is given by Findel, who, although a pronounced antagonist, shows very lucidly the underlying mystic basis on which the outward Masonic forms were supported, and it is of value to these researches to quote his testimony in full, illustrating, as it unwittingly does, the hypothesis put forward, namely, that all the societies similar to the African Brothers, the Fratres Lucis and others of like calibre, were but the outward manifestations of hidden forces which were attempting to indoctrinate the whole Masonic body with true spiritual, mental and moral mystic knowledge. Says Findel:

The Grand Lodge of Germany* further assumes,† that in the Building Fraternities ‡ of the Middle Ages, besides

---

* This Lodge "Zu den drei Weltkugeln" (The Three Globes) was established by Frederick II., who was its first Grand Master. It became the Grand Mother Lodge of Germany in 1744. It was also the protectress of the mystic element in Masonry for many years.

† Findel had been disputing the point held by the "Grand Lodge," *viz.*, that the links of true Masonry are to be found not in England, but in Scotland.

‡ "It has been argued with much force and apparent truth, that the building art was, in times of remotest antiquity, regarded as sacred, and existed under special concession and care of the native priesthood where it was practised, but this allegation cannot be accepted without qualification." Fort (George F.), *The Early History and Antiquities of Freemasonry*. Philadelphia, U.S.A., 1875, p. 363. And again, Mr. Fort tells us (p. 374) that in the years 643 and 729, "the inhabitants of Como had already attained to so high a degree of skill as to be designated *Magistri Comacini*, or Masters of Como." He further points out that their knowledge was obtained from the East, and directly from Byzantium, and then goes on to say "the secret arts thus obtained by the Teutonic races were perpetuated in fraternities or Guilds, whose existence ascends to the oldest forms of Germanic government."

their art, a secret science was carried on ; the substratum of which was a real Christian mystery, serving as a preparatory or elementary school and stepping-stone to that and the St. John's Masonry, which latter was not a mere system of moral philosophy, but closely allied and connected with this mystery. It was conceded that the Freemasonry of our days (St. John's Freemasonry) sprang from the Building Fraternities of the Middle Ages, but at the same time asserted that in the early ages there existed a secret society which strove to compass the perfecting of the human race, precisely in the same manner, and employing similar means, as did the Swedish system, which in fact only followed in the wake of its predecessor, being concealed in the Building Fraternities, so that our society did not rise from them, but made itself a way through them. The secret science, the mystery, was very ancient indeed. This mystery formed the secret of the Higher Degrees of the Rite, which were not merely kept hidden from the rest of the confederation, but also from the members of the inferior degrees of the system itself. This mystery was fully confirmed by documents, which the Grand Lodge of Germany had in its keeping. . . . . This secret legend is the same as that of the Carpocratians, which is that Jesus chose some of the Apostles and confided to them a secret science, which was transmitted afterwards to the priests of the Order of the Knights-Templars, and through them to the Building Fraternities, down to the present Freemasons of the Swedish Rite. . . . The Swedish system teaches that there have been men of all nations who have worshipped God in spirit and in truth, and surrounded by idolatry and superstition have yet preserved their purer faith. Separate from the world, and unknown to it, this Wisdom has been preserved by them and handed down as a mystery.

In the time of the Jews they had made use of the Essenes, in which sect Jesus was brought up, and had spent the greater part of his life. Having been instructed by him in a more perfect knowledge of holy things, they had amidst persecution taught in silence that which had been committed to their keeping.* At the period of the Saracens and the Crusades they were so greatly oppressed that they must ultimately have sought for protection from without. As fate, however, would have it, seven of them, Syriac Christians, pursued by unbelievers near Bastrum, were rescued by the Knights-Templars, and afterwards taken under their protection. When they had lived there for a certain time they begged for permission to dwell with the Canons or Prebendaries of Jerusalem, as the life there led agreed better with their own inclinations and habits. This was accorded them, and Andreas Montebarrensis effected a union of these Syrians with the Canons, to whom, out of gratitude, they imparted all their science, and so completely did they make the priests of the order the depositories of their secrets that they kept them and handed them over to others under certain conditions.

Thus, this secret knowledge, which was continually being added to, lived on in the very heart of the Order of Knights-Templars till its abolition. The clergy were dispersed with the persecution that ensued, but as the secular arm did not touch them as it did the Knights, they managed to rescue many of their secret writings, and when the Knights sought refuge in Scotland, they founded a chapter at Aberdeen, the first Prior of which was Petrus de Bononia. The science was disseminated from this place, but very cautiously, first to Italy, then to the extreme North (Sweden and Russia) and France. In Italy Abbot Severin had been the guardian of the True Science.†

---

* Compare with this statement, that a comparatively small body of men had received the inner teaching, and had a mission to hand it on, what was quoted about the "World-Wise Men" in the *Theosophical Review*, xxiii. 354.

† Findel (J. G.), *History of Freemasonry*, translated from the second German edition, by C. von Dalen, pp. 316-318. London, 1866.

Findel quotes all this history in a purely sceptical way, with adverse remarks of his own of doubt and derision. Nevertheless the history of this ancient secret teaching is true, and it coincides in its details with accounts which come to us from other sources. In order that the " hidden sources " may thus be more clearly kept in view, we will quote the words of a well-known Masonic writer, Mr. Lawrie:

Although it will be acknowledged by every unbiased reader, that Freemasonry has a wonderful resemblance to the Eleusinian and Dionysian mysteries, the fraternity of Ionian architects and the Essenian and Pythagorean associations, yet some may be disposed to question the identity of these institutions, because they had different names, and because some usages were observed by one which were neglected by another. But these circumstances of dissimilarity arise from those necessary changes which are superinduced upon every institution, by a spirit of innovation, by the caprice of individuals, and by the various revolutions in civilized society. Every alteration or improvement in philosophical systems, or ceremonial institutions, generally produces a corresponding variation in their name, deduced from the nature of the improvement, or from the name of the innovator.

The different associations, for example, whose nature and tendency we have been considering, received their names from circumstances merely casual, and often of trifling consideration ; though all of them were established for the same purpose, and derived from the same source. When the mysteries of the Essenes were imported by Pythagoras into Italy, without undergoing much variation, they were there denominated the mysteries of Pythagoras ; and, in our own day, they are called the secrets of Freemasonry, because many of their symbols are derived from the art of building, and because they are believed to have been invented by an association of architects, who were anxious to preserve, among themselves, the knowledge which they had acquired.*

The Dionysia, or Mysteries of Bacchus, were intimately connected with those of Ceres and perhaps still more with Freemasonry, says Mr. Lawrie; the rites came from Egypt, and there according to Plutarch Ceres was the Egyptian Isis, and Bacchus was Osiris.

The Dionysian artificers or architects were an association of scientific men, who were incorporated by command of the Kings of Pergamus into a corporate body, some three hundred years B.C. They had the city of Teos given to them. The members of this association which was intimately connected with the Dionysian mysteries, were distinguished from the uninitiated inhabitants of Teos, by their science, and by words and signs by which they could recognize their Brethren of the Order. Like Freemasons they were divided into Lodges which were characterised by different names.

From some circumstances which are stated in these inscriptions, but particularly from the name of one of the Lodges, it is highly probable that Attalus, King of Pergamus, was a member of the Dionysian Fraternity.

Such is the nature of that association of architects, who erected those splendid edifices in Ionia, whose ruins even afford us instruction, while they excite our surprise. If it be possible to prove the identity of any two societies, from the coincidence of their external forms, we are authorized to conclude that the Fraternity of the Ionian architects and the Fraternity of Freemasons, are exactly the same; and as the former practised the mysteries of Bacchus and Ceres,

---

* Symbols derived from the art of building, were also employed by the Pythagoreans, for conveying instruction to those who were initiated into their fraternity. See Proclus in Eucl. lib. XI. def. 2, etc.

several of which we have shown to be similar to the mysteries of Masonry, we may safely affirm, that, in their internal as well as external procedure, the Society of Freemasons resembles the Dionysiacs of Asia Minor.

The opinion, therefore, of Freemasons, that their Order existed, and flourished at the building of Solomon's Temple, is by no means so pregnant with absurdity, as some men would wish us to believe.

We have already shown, from authentic sources of information, that the mysteries of Ceres and Bacchus were instituted about four hundred years before the reign of Solomon; * and there are strong reasons for believing that even the association of the Dionysian architects existed before the building of the Temple.

It was not, indeed, till about three hundred years before the birth of Christ, that they were incorporated at Teos, under the Kings of Pergamus; but it is universally allowed, that they arose long before their settlement in Ionia, and, what is more to our present purpose, that they existed in the very land of Judea.

The difference in the ceremonial observances of these institutions, may be accounted for nearly upon the same principles. From the ignorance, or superior sagacity of those who presided over the ancient fraternities, some ceremonies would be insisted upon more than others, some of less moment would be exalted into consequence, while others of greater importance would be depressed into obscurity. In process of time, therefore, some trifling changes would be effected upon these ceremonies, some rites abolished, and some introduced. The chief difference, however, between the ancient and modern mysteries, is in

---

* According to Playfair's Chronology, the Temple of Solomon was begun in 1016 and finished in 1008, B.C. The Eleusinian mysteries were introduced into Athens in 1356, B.C., a considerable time after their institution.

those points which concern religion. But this arises from the great changes which have been produced in religious knowledge. It cannot be supposed that the rites of the Egyptian, Jewish, and Grecian religions should be observed by those who profess only the religion of Christ; or that we should pour out libations to Ceres and Bacchus, who acknowledge no heavenly superior, but the true and the living God.*

The connection† of the Afrikanische Bauherren with the Templars and their secret traditions is common to all those mystic associations‡ who

---

* Lawrie, (Alexander), *The History of Freemasonry, drawn from authentic sources of information, with an account of the Grand Lodge of Scotland*, p. 28 *et seq.* Edinburgh, 1804.

† They have both a common bond in Manichæism, the Templars were "Sons of the Widow" in the earlier times, as well as the African Brothers. Both bodies again hold the Egyptian line of tradition, and were versed in its grand symbology and hieroglyph.—Lenning (C.). *Allgemeines Handbuch der Freimaurerei*, I., p. 7. Leipzig, 1863.

‡ "There is no portion of our annals so worthy of investigation as that which is embraced by the middle ages of Christendom when the whole of Europe was perambulated by our Brethren, in associations of travelling artizans, under the name of 'Free and Accepted Masons,' for the purpose of erecting religious edifices. There is not a country of Europe, which does not at this day contain honourable evidences of the skill and industry of our Masonic ancestors. I therefore propose, in the present article, to give a brief sketch of the origin, the progress, and the character of these travelling architects. Clavel, in his *Histoire Pittoresque de la Franc-Maçonnerie*, has traced the organization of these associations to the *collegia artificum*, or colleges of artisans, which were instituted at Rome by Numa, in the year B.C. 714, and whose members were originally Greeks, imported by this law-giver for the purpose of embellishing the city over which he reigned. These associations existed in Rome in the time of the Emperors. They were endowed with certain privileges peculiar to themselves, such as a government by their own statutes, the power of making contracts as a corporation, and an immunity from taxation. Their meetings were held in private, like the esoteric schools of the philosophers. Their presiding officers were called

claimed, like them, to have deeper truths and more spiritual knowledge in charge for the human race.

Seeing, then, that the African Brothers have this link with other mystic bodies, we can investigate the details of their system with interest, and we find that the members of this school were almost without exception learned men and persons of position and rank, often selected by the King as suitable members. Devoted to mystic research, in general they paid the closest attention to symbolism and hieroglyphs.

The description given of them by Ragon differs somewhat in detail to that given by Lenning, which runs as follows:

The double character of the Order confirms what we know about the tendency and ritual of the first four grades. They are as follows:

Grade 1. Pupil of the Egyptian secrets (Menes Musæ).*
Here the doctrines of the true Religion, as concealed under the hieroglyphs which were already in the Egyptian Mysteries, were brought forward for the pupil. The first degree shows already that Moses was held as an important teacher of these doctrines even to the Egyptians.

Grade 2. The Initiates of the Ægæic secrets. Here Moses was presented as one of the greatest of the Wise Men of the world, who instructed the Jews in the

---

"magistri." They were divided into three classes, corresponding with the three degrees of Freemasonry, and they admitted into their ranks as honorary members persons who were not by profession operative Masons. Finally, they used a symbolic language drawn from the implements of masonry, and they were in possession of a secret mode of recognition."—Mackey's *Lexicon of Freemasonry*. Charleston, 1845, p. 316.

* Ragon gives "Manes" where Lenning uses "Menes."

doctrines of religion from his knowledge of nature and the world.

Grade 3. The Cosmopolitans (or citizens of the world) had for its object the necessity for self-knowledge, because most ethical teachers failed in teaching this, for they depicted all human nature as being utterly corrupt, while instead of this, human nature was capable through self-knowledge of, and self-respect for, its destiny, of becoming a great instrument for the work of God.

Grade 4. The Christian world-wise men (or Bossonians) —was the expounding of the intimate connection between man and the world, so that to call each of them the 'Temple,' and to call Christ the Foundation Stone was the True Religion.

Grade 5. Was practically that of the Alethophiles, or Friends of Truth, which was identical with the society of that name, and whose tendency is expressed in the name.

After these five, or lower student-grades, there follow three higher, or inner grades, of which, however, only the names are known in the outer world. According to what is told, they were the same as the Freimaurerei Ritterwesen. . . . The names are variously given and are of but little consequence, this Order was never a very large one, for the qualifications as to learning and education were somewhat restrictive at that period. It appears to have had its Lodges in Berlin, and also in Oberlavsitz; there were some of the same Lodges in Cologne, Worms, and also in Paris under the guidance of a certain Kühn. He came into contact with Baron von Hund and his system of 'The Strict Observance' of which Von Köppen was a devoted member.*

The brief mention of the highest grade, the Knights of Silence, or Everlasting Silence, is

---

* Lenning (C.), *Allgemeines Handbuch der Freimaurerei*, pp. 7-8. Leipzig, 1863.

interesting, for it has reference to an edict which was published from the "Unknown Heads" suspending all studies and all work for a time—the limit of time was not specified. There will be more, however, to be said on this point at a later date. The Minister of War, Herr von Köppen, was aided in his work of organisation in the African Brothers by Herr von Hymmen, a Councillor of Justice in Berlin; both men were Rosicrucians, and von Hymmen was an adherent of the Baron von Gugomas, another celebrated mystic in the last century.

Von Köppen and von Hymmen published the well-known work, *Crata Repoa, or Initiation in the Ancient Secret Society of the Egyptian Priests.**

Another leader of this confraternity was Karl du Bosc, one of the chamberlains at the Prussian Court. He was also connected with the Rosicrucians and some of the other mystic sects. It confirms the accuracy of our hypothesis when we find all these public officers working harmoniously in different organizations, aiding all for the general weal, knowing well that each Society represented, as it were, one facet of the precious stone of truth which lay hidden securely beneath the surface.

Turning now to the links which connect the African Brothers with other mystic fraternities we shall find the Deutsche Ritter, or Kreuz-Herren, akin to them; the origin of the last-mentioned association

---

* *Crata Repoa, oder Einweihungen in der alten geheimen Gesellschaft der Aegyptien Priester.* Berlin, 1770.

HIDDEN SOURCES OF MASONRY. 71

can be traced back to the year 1190, where their history is closely allied with another interesting body, *viz.*, the Maltheser-Ritter, or Knights of Malta; coalescing again with these we find the well-known Johanniter-Ritter, or Knights of St. John, whose history is so intimately interwoven with the Johannite Masonry, dedicated as it was to the two St. John's, the Baptist and the Evangelist.

Further, we find a curious secret sect existing in Africa of which Mollien gives a most interesting sketch. He calls this sect "Les Almousseri," and connects their community with the Freemasons as follows :

In Foutatoro, and among the Moors, there exists a sort of freemasonry, the secret of which has never been revealed; the adept is shut up for eight days in a hut, he is allowed to eat but once a day, he sees no person excepting the slave appointed to carry him his food; at the end of that period a number of men in masks present themselves, and employ all possible means to put his courage to the proof; if he acquits himself with honour he is admitted. The initiated pretend that at this moment they are enabled to behold all the kingdoms of the earth, that the future is unveiled to them, and that thenceforward heaven grants all their prayers. In the villages where persons of this fraternity reside, they perform the functions of conjurors, and are called Almousseri. One day Boukari told me, after attesting the truth of what he was about to say by the most solemn oaths, that being in a canoe with one of these men, there fell such a heavy shower of rain that he would not depart; yielding, however, to the wishes of the Almousseri, he set sail; "torrents of rain fell on all sides," added Boukari, "but our bark remained perfectly dry, and a favourable wind swelled our sails. I asked this Almousseri to explain his secret, but he answered that if he revealed it his brethren would infallibly destroy him."*

From many sources it is evident that scattered communities † with mystic knowledge, existed in various parts of Northern Africa. Such communities having nothing to do, of course, with the fetish-worship of the negro tribes, but adhere to the Egyptian tradition of mystic teaching, for they are off-shoots of the Manichæan and Coptic teachers who spread the secret doctrines of Manes in Northern Africa; his disciples carried on this line of work immediately after his death. They kept up also a communication with the mystics in Europe, for M. de St. Germain at one period of his travels was in Northern Africa.

Some reference has been made to the fifth grade of the African Bauherren system, namely the "Master of the Egyptian Secrets"; "Alethophilote" or "Friend of Truth." This grade is given as the eighth by Ragon,‡ and Lenning in his encyclopædia says:

There appears to have been some connection between this grade and the little known society of the "Alethophilotes" in Berlin. This is probably the earlier sect which

---

* Mollien (G.), *Travels in the Interior of Africa*, translated from the French, edited by T. E. Bowdich, p. 161. London, 1820.

† These communities were chiefly Moors and Arabians, and we touch the Sufite mystic tradition along this line.

‡ See *The Theosophical Review*, xxiii., 358.

is alluded to sometimes, and it was founded, so far as is known, by the Graf von Manteuffel in 1736.*

The details of this system will be of interest to students, as it throws some light upon the older association, of which very little is told; they are given by Kundmann as follows:

I. Let Truth be the sole aim of your understanding and of your will.

II. Consider nothing true, consider nothing false, if you are not convinced about it by adequate reasons.

III. Be satisfied with this, that you know and love the Truth; seek to impart it, that is to make it known and agreeable to your fellow-citizens. He who buries his experience, buries a thing which has been committed to his care for the furtherance of the glory of the Highest; and he thus diverts its use from humanity, which might have profited therefrom.

IV. Do not deny your love and help to those who know the Truth and are seeking it themselves, or who are honestly trying to defend it. It would be too disgraceful and contrary to the actual vocation of an Alethophilote (Friend of Truth) if you were to deny protection and defence to those whose object is one with yours.

V. Never contradict a truth when you see that you are being overborne by others whose insight is more keen than yours. An Alethophilote would be unworthy of his name if he undertook to combat the Truth out of pride or conceit, or from any other unreasonable cause.

VI. Be pitiful with those who either are ignorant of the Truth, or who have incorrect perceptions of it; instruct

---

* Lenning (C.), *Allegemeines Handbuch der Freimaurerei*, i., 15. Leipzig, 1863.

them without bitterness, and seek to bring them into the right way solely by the strength of your arguments and by no other way. You would disgrace the Truth and make it appear suspicious if you were to fight for it and defend it with any other weapons but those which Reason gives into your hand.*

It is an interesting, but somewhat difficult, matter to understand the reason why such bitter war was carried on against bodies of men with tenets so high and aims so pure. As each of these semi-Masonic sects is investigated the astonishment of the student increases at the groundless accusations with which the ordinary historian is content.

In the passage quoted from Findel, he gives the traditions and Masonic tenets held by the Grand Lodge of Germany, and also by the Afrikanische Bauherren, these bodies being practically identical, the latter being but a more advanced and occult section of the Mother-Lodge. In the passage just referred to the Carpocratians are particularly alluded to; this Gnostic sect is of especial interest to students of Theosophy, seeing that metempsychosis —or re-incarnation—was one of their tenets; and if we summarise a well-known authority on the subject we get an identity of view which is remarkable.

These sectarians called themselves Gnostics. In most respects the teaching of their Founder coincides with that of Basilides. He held there was one principal virtue from

---

*Kundmann, *Die höhen und niedern Schulen Deutschlands*, p. 769. Breslau, 1741.

whom proceeded all other virtues and angels who founded this world ; that Jesus Christ was not born of a virgin, but a man truly born of the seed of Joseph, though better than other men in integrity of Life. . . Virtue was given Him by the Great First Cause whereby He retained the recollection of things seen in a former state of existence. . . . Metempsychosis and the pre-existence of the soul was an integral part of the system.*

There is much more of interest in the summary given for the student of Modern Gnosticism or Theosophia, and it can also be readily seen that if the tenets of the Carpocratians were held by the African Brothers, the Templars and other mystic sects, then there was indeed a vital necessity for secrecy and silence, since these heretical views brought about the destruction of the Templars in the Middle Ages, and would have called forth the direst wrath not only of the Catholic, but also the Protestant authorities.

---

* Blunt (John Henry, D.D.), *Dictionary of Sects and Heresies*, p. 102. London, 1891. See also Mead (G. R. S.), "Among the Gnostics of the First Two Centuries," *Lucifer*, xx. 207.

THE TRADITIONS OF THE TEMPLARS REVIVED IN MASONRY.

THE RITE OF THE STRICT OBSERVANCE.

ANCIENT history is like a night-landscape, over which we grope, vaguely discerning a few outlines in the general gloom, and happy if here or there the works of a particular author or a ruin or work of art momentarily illumine, like a lightning flash in the dark, the particular field which we are exploring. — *Philo about the Contemplative Life*, p. 349, F. C. CONYBEARE.

DUPES or charlatans! Such is the stricture of the Masonic authorities on the leading spirits of the Strict Observance; but as the student wades through the pile of polemical literature which has heaped itself round this particular body, he is moved to ask: Is it possible that all the honesty and wisdom is with the critics; and is it rational to suppose that in this widespread development of mystic Masonry there existed no one clear-sighted enough to do within the body the work which the "enemy at the gate" ever arrogates to himself as his special function, the work of healthy investigation?

One well-known authority opens fire with the following critical broadside:

Of all the wonderful perversions of Freemasonry which owe their origin to the fervid imaginings of our brethren of the last century, none can compare in point of interest with the system of the "Strict Observance."* . . . The whole system was based upon the fiction that at the time of the destruction of the Templars, a certain number of Knights took refuge in Scotland, and there preserved the existence of the Order. The sequence of Grand-Masters was presumed never to have been broken, and a list of those rulers in regular succession was known to the initiates, but the identity of the actual Grand-Master was always kept during his life-time a secret from everyone except his immediate confidants—hence the term "Unknown Superiors."

In order to secure their perfect security these Knights are said to have joined the Guilds of Masons in Scotland, and thus to have given rise to the Fraternity of Freemasons.†

The trail of the materialistic serpent is traceable in his valuable work, although the author is in advance

---

* "The mysteries of Mithras were solemnized in a consecrated cavern, on December 25th, which was the date fixed for the celebration. They began from the moment that the priests at midnight saw the constellation of Virgo appear, which on setting ushered in the year by calling forth the sun, which appeared as a son supporting itself on its Mother's lap.

"Some Masonic Systems have preserved the Magian degree, it is the last in the Strict Observance." Acerrellos (R. S.), *Die Freimaurerei in ihrem Zusammenhange mit den Religionen der alten Aegypter, der Juden, und der Christen*, I., p. 293. Leipzig, 1836.

† Gould (R. F.), *Hist. of Freemasonry.* V., p. 99. London, 1886.

of some German critics by giving credit for honest motives to one at least of the leaders of this Rite. But even with this extension of generosity it is evident that "dupes or charlatans" is the summing up by at least two-thirds of the Masonic writers in the last century and in the present one, of the mental and moral condition of the members of the Strict Observance.

The evidences of the position—mental, moral and worldly—of many of the members, however, preclude such a hasty generalisation, for it should not be overlooked by critics who thus stigmatise the students of mysticism that more royalties, members of reigning families, scholars and officers, belonged to this Order, than were enrolled on any other Masonic list. And among these princes and grand-dukes were earnest students, good and wise rulers, men respected by all who knew them both for their judgment and their probity. With them we find scholars, nobles and officers of high standing, with stainless records; these again cannot be swept up into one category or the other, and even allowing for a residue of members whose principles were not of the highest, and making a generous allowance for such persons, who are found in every society, even then there remains too large a body of honest members devoted to mystic research to allow of any hasty generalisations, and the fact remains of a widespread feeling that within Masonry was hidden that occult and mystic tradition which is the true history of spiritual evolution.

THE TEMPLARS. 79

In reading the merciless and shallow criticisms upon those members of the Strict Observance who were trying to re-assert the mystic doctrine, it is amusing to note the cool assumptions of honesty and clear-sightedness which—from their own stand-point—appear to have been the sole prerogatives of an all-knowing few who had sounded—as they thought—mysticism and its supernatural follies with an illuminated wisdom that angels might envy.

Before passing to the system itself, however, it will be well to note some of the members who have fallen under the " mangling tooth of criticism." We find in the year 1774 no less than twelve reigning princes were members of this Rite, and in the list which follows—in which by no means all the royal members are cited—we find that in some cases whole families joined the Society. They cannot all have been dupes, and they were certainly not charlatans; they were also in too responsible positions for them to have taken up with what was doubtful. The list stands as follows:

Karl George, Landgraf of Hesse-Darmstadt.

Friedrich, Landgraf and Prince of Hesse-Kassel.

Ludwig, Grand-Duke and Prince of Hesse-Darmstadt.

Christian Ludwig, Landgraf and Prince of Hesse-Darmstadt.

Friedrich George August, Prince of Hesse-Darmstadt.

Ludwig George, Prince of Hesse-Darmstadt.

Friedrich Karl Alexander, Markgraf of Brandenburg, Onolzbach and Baireuth.

Karl I., Duke of Brunswick, and his three sons:

Friedrich August, Maximilian Julius Leopold, Wilhelm Adolf.

Karl, Grand-Duke of Mecklenburg-Strelitz.

Karl, Prince of Hesse-Kassel.

Karl, Prince of Courland.

These are a few of those who joined this much decried Rite, and the same class of members may be found in Austria, Italy, France, Russia, and Sweden. All, moreover, were real lovers of mysticism; many of them were members of the Rosicrucian and other allied bodies, all were seeking in various systems for the old narrow path which leads to wisdom; not seeking by one way alone, but testing all ways that presented themselves. A sketch, therefore, of some of the leading spirits in this interesting Order may perhaps be of interest, and it will serve to bring the leading spirits more clearly before our readers.

The most important personage is Charles Gotthelf, Baron of the Holy Roman Empire, of Hund and Alten-Grotkare, a Lusatian nobleman, born in 1722. He became, in 1753, a Royal Polish and Electoral Saxon Chamberlain, and in 1755 was elected senior of the nobility of Upper Lusatia. The seven years' war brought great misfortune to him, his estates being occupied and plundered by the war-waging armies. He had himself, as an adherent of Austria, to flee to Bohemia, where he remained until the end of the war. King Augustus of Poland appointed him a Privy Councillor in 1769, and Maria Theresa in that year

THE TEMPLARS. 81

did the same; but he did not accept the post in Vienna, being desirous of accomplishing the contemplated reform of Masonry.

He entered the Masonic Order in 1742, when at Frankfurt-am-Main. In the next year he is said to have established a Lodge at Paris, and while staying with the French Army he became acquainted with the heads of a Rite which pretended to be, in its higher degrees, the continuation of the famous Order of Knights Templars. According to his repeated declarations, maintained even on his death-bed, he was received into this Order in Paris by Lord Kilmarnock, Grand-Master of Scotland, a Jacobite nobleman, on which occasion Lord Clifford acted as Prior. He was presented to a very high member of the Order, a mysterious personage called only "the Knight of the Red Feather." Perhaps this was Prince Charles Edward himself. Von Hund supposed him to be the Supreme Grand Master of the Order, and was appointed by him coadjutor of the Seventh Province of the Order (Germania Inferior). Hund visited Scotland also, where he was bidden to raise the Order in Germany, together with the then Master of the Seventh Province, de Marschall, whom he always considered his predecessor. Marschall had founded Lodges at Altenburg and Naumburg, but found only in the latter men worthy of being led further, *viz.*, to be received into the Templar degrees. He did not care for the rest of the German Lodges, and on his return to Germany (about 1751) Hund placed himself in connection with Marschall, who, unfortunately, was very ill already, and died soon afterwards.

Before his death he destroyed nearly all his Templar papers, only a very few of which he had given to Hund. He (Hund) hoped to find the missing rituals, etc., with the Naumburg Lodge, but was disappointed. He, therefore, sent two brethren of that Lodge to England and Scotland, in order to acquire the missing documents. They returned, carrying with them only a patent to him as Master of the Seventh Province, written in cypher, and nothing more.*

A full account of the working arrangements of the Order is given by the writer from whom we summarise, and he tells us these were changed from time to time according to the conditions that arose incident upon the constant attacks that were being made on this and all other occult societies by the group of materialists in Germany, Herr Dr. Biester and his colleagues, of whom mention has already been made,† and there will be necessity to refer to these critics again a little later on. Another interesting sketch of the Baron von Hund by Reghellini runs as follows:

In 1756 the wars had caused the Prussian (Masonic) Lodges to be abandoned. Baron de Hund, who had received the High Templar's Degree in the Chapter of Clermont at Paris, on returning to Berlin declared that he had been raised to the dignity of Grand-Master of the Templars by M. Marschall, who called himself the successor of the G ∴ G ∴ Master-Templars by uninterrupted transmission from the time of Jacques Molay; that Marschall on his death-bed had delegated this high dignity to him, and had declared him his successor, transmitting to him all his powers and dignities. He did not omit to give Hund a list of all the names of the Templar Grand-Masters, which must therefore have been a curious contrast to the list of the Order of the Temple of Paris.

---

* This summary is taken from an interesting study on the Baron von Hund, written by a well-known Hungarian mason, which appeared in the *Ars Quatuor Coronatorum*, "Transactions of the Lodge Quatuor Coronati," No. 2076. VI., part ii., p. 89. Margate, 1893.

† *The Theosophical Review*, xxii. p. 431.

Hund placed himself at the head of the German reformers: he persuaded them that his Rite would restore Freemasonry ∴ to its ancient brilliancy and its former splendour; he was even bold enough to establish, at his own expense, a Lodge at Kittlitz, near Löbau. At the same time he caused a Protestant church to be built. It was the Brother Masons of this Lodge who laid the first stone; Baron de Hund placed upon this stone a copper plate on which he had his Masonic ∴ opinions engraved, and if we except that of the continuation of the Ancient Templar Order in the Masonry ∴ to which he especially belonged (for in order to be received into the Rite of the Clerks of the Strict Observance he had even become a Catholic*)—if we except, as we say, this opinion, we believe that his principles were altogether philosophical. In the doctrines of his *Eques Professus*, the eighth rung which he added to the Templar ladder of the Strict Observance, he maintains that these Pontiffs are the only Priests of the True Light, the Worshippers of God, and the disciples of the pure doctrines of Jesus and of John.†

There are very many details about the work done by Von Hund in his efforts to draw the mystic side of Masonry into prominence; details which can be read in the work of any real authority on the history of Masonry, and which cannot, for want of space, be entered into in these pages. Most of the German Masonic authorities, such as Keller, Rebold, Krause, Lenning, Findel, and others, concede his personal asceticism and moreover his entire honesty of purpose, but he is usually summed up as a dupe.

---

* This is contradicted by some authorities.

† Reghellini da Schio (Par le F ∴ M ∴ R ∴ da S ∴), *La Maçonnerie considerèe comme le Resultat des Religions égyptienne, juive et chrétienne*, II., pp. 374, 375. Paris, 1833.

Passing on to another aspect of this much-tangled web of Masonic evolution, we find that about 1770 events of great importance transpired in Germany; Duke Ferdinand of Brunswick had become a Mason, and he induced his brother, the reigning Duke Charles, and his nephews—the sons of Duke Charles —to enter the Masonic Fraternity, and they all joined the Rite of the Strict Observance. It was at this juncture that there appeared also on the scene Johann Augustus Starck, a profoundly striking personality from all accounts.

He had been in St. Petersburg from 1762-65 as teacher of Oriental languages, and was also a deep student of theology and philosophy. Starck had held many public positions of trust and importance, amongst others that of interpreter of Oriental MSS. at the Royal Library in Paris. He had travelled in England, Scotland, Italy and Russia, and was an ardent searcher after hermetic and theosophic mysticism. In St. Petersburg he had come into contact with the Melesino System, which was both hermetic and theosophic in its tenets.

Starck held that the mystic traditions of the Knights-Templars, derived by them from those still older fraternities with whom they had been in contact in the East, were preserved amongst the clericals of that Order who had cherished their unbroken continuity until his days, and he announced that he was in communication with certain Superiors, or chiefs of the Order.

THE TEMPLARS.

Our well-known English authority, writing on the Strict Observance, says:

On February 17th, 1767, some Masons, chief amongst whom may be mentioned Von Vegesack, Von Bohnen and Starck, founded at Wismar the Lodge of the "Three Lions," and added thereto a Scots Lodge, "Gustavus of the Golden Hammer."

Shortly afterwards they added a hitherto unknown body, a "Clerical Chapter." To these brethren we are indebted for the historical fiction *(sic)* that the Knights-Templars were divided into military and sacerdotal members; that the latter possessed all the secrets and mystic learning of the Order; and that they had preserved a continuous existence down to the eighteenth century. Starck claimed to be the emissary of these Clerical Templars, asserted their and his superiority over the Secular Knights, and offered, on his claims being acknowledged, to impart their valuable secrets to Von Hund and his disciples. Starck (1741—1816), was a student of Göttingen, and a very learned man, an Oriental linguist of great attainments, and had held scientific appointments in St. Petersburg, Paris, Wismar, and elsewhere.*

The author of this work—a standard work on Masonry—regards Starck as a charlatan, although he brings no proofs, other than his assertions, which are upheld by many modern materialistic critics, that there were no leaders, or unknown Superiors, that the tradition was false, and that no real connection existed between the Templars and the Masons. Unfortunately for many of these critics this tradition was not "written in the stars" but preserved on stones, and we find the eminent archæologist Baron

---

* Gould, *Hist. of Freemasonry*, V., p. 104. London, 1886.

Joseph von Hammer* demonstrating the connection between the Masons and the Templars. He traces the Eastern origin of both by means of engraved symbols, showing the extraordinary identity between those used by the Masons, and those of the Templars, and practically makes them identical in their inception, that is to say, developed from the same original stock of mystic Eastern lore, and when we have to sketch the history of the Knights-Templars we shall turn to these researches for their monumental records, proving the Eastern sources from which the secret traditions of the Templars were derived; justifying the claim of all those later societies which based their assertions on the same tradition.

At present we must confine ourselves to the Strict Observance, and so we pass on to what Johann Starck says in his own writings on the subject. One of his works deals entirely with the accusation brought against the Strict Observance and other secret societies, namely that they were derived from the Jesuit order.†

He was particularly attacked on his belief that the Knights-Templars could have continued in existence for four hundred and fifty years, unknown to the world at large. To this charge he replied that

If he [Dr. Biester‡] had been somewhat better

---

* *Fundgruben des Orients*, VI., p. 445 (Wien, 1818), "Gegenrede wider die Einrede der Vertheidiger der Templer."

† See his long dissertation on the subject in *Uber Krypto Katholicismus, Proselyten-Macherey, Jesuitismus, Geheime Gesellschaften*, etc. Frankfort und Leipzig, 1787.

‡ Editor of the *Berliner Monatschrift*. See above, p. 13.

acquainted with ecclesiastical history, he would have found not only one, but several religious bodies, which under far more violent oppression and persecution than those endured by the Knights-Templars, have secretly continued to exist for a longer period than four hundred and fifty years.

Starck's view is upheld by a modern writer of note, who, speaking of the Templars says:

Considering how widely the Order had spread its branches, obtained possession and affiliated to itself multitudes both male and female amongst the laity all over Europe, it would be a mere absurdity to believe that all its traditions were swept away at one stroke by the suppression of the Templars in the year 1307.*

Thus we find this view supported a century later than the time when Starck penned his defence of the tradition. Starck proceeds, moreover, to show how many scholars were of the same opinion. He writes:

How great are the number of scholars who joined it [the Strict Observance] and accepted the opinion that the order of the Templars had continued to exist for four hundred and fifty years, secretly truly, but uninterruptedly! There are Professor Dähmart at Greifswalde, *Eques ab abiete*, Doctor and Professor Rehfeld, *Eques à caprea*, Doctor and Professor Rölpen, *Eques à tribus specis*, Professor and Preacher Ruhlenkamp at Göttingen, *Eques à gallo cantante*, Professor Schwarz at Reval, *Eques à rota*, Professor Eck at Leipzig, *Eques à noctua*, etc.

These men are scholars and students holding responsible public positions and as such would hardly be all fools or charlatans. Space will not permit us

---

* King (C.W.), *The Gnostics and their Remains, Ancient and Mediæval*, p. 399, 2nd ed. London, 1887.

to follow at present all the arguments brought forward by Starck, in order to show the absurdity of the accusations of Jesuitism, an accusation which was freely brought against many of the societies of the period; we must pass on to the condition of the society itself, and trace even this but briefly.

Ragon, in speaking of the Strict Observance, says that in Germany a society was formed of Reformed Masons, that is to say:

> Approaching more nearly to the true institution than the ordinary Freemasons. The study of the Kabala, of the Philosopher's Stone, and of Necromancy or the invocation of spirits, occupied them chiefly, because according to them all these sciences formed the system and the object and end of the ancient mysteries of which Freemasonry is the sequel.*

The studies enumerated in this quotation appear to have been carried on chiefly in one of the higher grades of the Strict Observance called *Clerici Ordinis Templariorum*. It was this branch that took up the study of Alchemy, and which was under the particular direction of Starck, Herr von Raven, and others, who were entirely devoted to the mystic side of Masonry. Ragon gives the following divisions and grades into which the System was divided, namely:

1. Apprenti
2. Compagnon
3. Maître
4. Maître Écossais
5. Novice

} Symboliques.

---

* Ragon (J. M.), *Orthodoxie Maçonnique*, p. 210. Paris, 1853.

6. Templier, divisé en 3 classes sous les noms de } Eques. Socius. Armiger.

Between 1768 and 1770 the Baron von Hund added a seventh grade, which he called :

7. Eques Professus.

It is also stated by Ragon* that the largest portion of this society became Martinists, and were known later by the name of the "Knights of the Holy Sepulchre." This change was made at the convention at Lyons, which took place in 1778. The Duke Ferdinand of Brunswick and the Baron von Raven also joined this division. Another group took the name of the "Beneficent Knights of the Holy City," and amongst them we find the two mystics, the Comte de St. Martin and Willermoz.

It will be better to add here a few details about the Knights Templars, since they are so intimately connected with the Masonic Order just mentioned ; details which will also serve to show the inner aspect of their tradition. Much has been written about them and their history—from one aspect—is better known than that of almost any other mystic organisation, but the fact of a secret teaching is not sufficiently clear. That there was a secret doctrine†

---

* *Op. cit.*, p. 230.

† If these facts already point to the existence of secret statutes in the Order of the Knights Templars, this will also be proved by a number of other notes and finally substantiated by some quite positive statements which are most explicit.

A great number of witnesses, who give information on the

amongst the Templars is shown by Neaf*; he points out that the Knights Templars considered that the Roman Church had failed in its ideal, and that when the terrible persecutions fell upon them that they divided and joined two different associations, one the body of Freemasons and the other a body named the Johannites. Another writer† points out the connection between the Templars and the Bogomiles, who were the Manichæans of the Balkan Provinces, and the Gnostics of the early Christian period and their descendants, the Cathari of the mediæval ages. Dr. Simrock‡ suggests a deeply interesting idea with regard to the connection between the tradition of the Holy Grail and the secret teachings of the Templars; he appears to consider that the Grail tradition, which is drawn in some parts from the Apocryphal Gospels, is the basis of the secret teaching of the Templars. Some of the early sources of the tradition are given

---

ceremonies of admission in question refer the same to certain definite phrases which describe them. It then furthermore transpires that these secret statutes were not only received by means of oral tradition but also existed in manuscript form. Gervais de Beauvais saw at one of the Heads of the Orders, a little book with the Statutes of the Order of 1128, which was shown without thinking, and he knew that the same man had also possessed another book about which he was very mysterious and which he "would not show anyone for all the world." Prutz (Hans Dr.), *Geheimelehre des Templherren Ordens*, p. 45. Berlin, 1879.

* Naef (F.), *Recherches sur les Opinions religieuses des Templiers*, pp. 25 to 41. Nismes, 1890.

† Loiseleur (Jules), *La Doctrine Secrète des Templiers*, pp. 35, 48. Paris, 1872.

‡ Simrock (Dr. K.), *Parzifal u. Titurel, Rittergedichte von Wolfram von Eschenbach*, I., 497. Stuttgart und Tübingen, 1842.

THE TEMPLARS. 91

by the author of Sarsena, and also the connection between the Templars and the Essenes.

All these links are of importance if we wish to understand the close connection between these various organizations, and also how one developed out of the other. Another writer says:

Taking the rules of their Order and of the Christians in equal division, they (the Kabalists) began to draw a parallel between the books of Moses and the records of the Magi, and formed from all this material a new Brotherhood into which they imported certain rules that could exist together with those of the Christians. During the Crusades there were several orders of widely different views; and among numerous others in the year 1118, the Knights of the Temple, with whom the Magi joined themselves, and to whom they imparted their principles and mysteries. The fall of the Templars and the entire demolition of the Order by the Council held in Vienna in 1311, is due to the fact that all the knowledge which we may consider as part of the Wisdom of the ancient Magi, and also the Natural Sciences, had at this time begun to be lost. There is one section of Freemasons which finds in Freemasonry the restoration of the Order of the Knights Templars, and the systems of the Great German Lodge and that of the Swedish Brothers are certainly pre-eminently connected with the former. According to this system, and in especial according to all the various systems which obtain in this particular Order, Freemasonry is a mystical conception of the principle doctrines of Christianity, the slain Master no other than the Christ! And here the question fairly arises, had the teachings of the Christ in truth mysteries, unsearchable, incomprehensible doctrines, which were only to be made comprehensible to a small number of specially chosen disciples, and were not the Essenes that body among whom He had learned those mysteries, for the Essenes demanded of those initiated, moderation, justice, avoidance of injury, love of Truth and detestation of evil; holy water belonged to the ritual of admission to their highest grade, and John said "Repent and be baptized." Christ who led the blameless life, suffered himself to be baptized. Does not this lead us to the almost certain conclusion that Christ, and even more John, were initiated members of the Essenes? Were sufficient documents available to prove the historic truth of this statement, it would be perfectly obvious why John (the Baptist) who bled for Truth and Goodness, should have been chosen as the Patron of the present Order and of nearly all that precede it. The keeping of John the Baptist's Day as a Festival by the Freemasons is adduced in confirmation of this idea that the Freemasons had for over six hundred years identified themselves with the "Johannrittern" and St. John the Baptist had been chosen Patron by both Orders. And as it is certain that much of the ritual of the form of Reception means something quite other than that which has been substituted latterly, it may very easily be that there is some truth in this assertion. For it is just as little true that the Freemasons identified themselves six hundred years ago with the "Johannrittern" as that they now crown the Master, Hiram, in the Lodge in real earnest. Christ, as has been said above, founded no secret society, and yet He gave out His teaching only by degrees as regarded its inner significance, for he said "I have many things to say unto you, but ye cannot bear them now." After His death the pure doctrine was falsified by additions, but yet it may be possible that its pristine purity and simplicity may have been preserved, and where else than in some kind of Order? In the early Christian Church there was a *disciplina arcani*, and in this manner were the mysteries transmitted among the few, and even in the time of the Crusades there were still living descendants of the Essenes. The Order of Knights of the Temple was founded in the year 1113 by Gottfried

THE TEMPLARS.

von St. Omar, Hugo de Paiens, and seven others whose names are not known. They consecrated themselves to the service of God according to the form of the *Canonicorum Regularium*, and took solemn vows before the Bishop of Jerusalem. Baldwin the Second, in consideration of the office of these seven servants of God, lent to them a house near the Temple of Solomon. They bound themselves (as we are told by the author of the book called *Die theoretische Brüder* U.S.V.) with certain Essenes who formed a secret society consisting of virtuous Christians and true seekers after Truth in Nature, and learned also their secrets. That the Templars had mysteries in their keeping is beyond contention. The Order had secret ceremonies of admission, gloried in possessing such, and for this reason several of its members endured martyrdom. The Order of Knights Templar contained many of the best and most far-seeing minds among the parents of Freemasonry; and, as is well-known, there were whole branches of Freemasonry specially devoted to the restoration of the Templars. And the Johannine and other systems taught this descent, even before the "Strict Observance" became generally known, which insisted on the restoration of the Templars as the highest aim of the mysteries. If we consider closely the similarity between the customs of both Orders we shall find that the Reception and other ceremonies of the Order of Freemasonry relates to that of the Knights of the Temple exactly in so far as to enable us to say with positiveness that the Freemasons preserve in their midst the mysteries of the Templars and transmit them. That the Templars possessed secrets is witnessed by the evidence in their procedure: the Freemasons claim the like procedure for themselves, for from grade to grade the Aspirant is told that later he shall experience yet more. More what? Also a secret. Nine Brothers founded the Order of the Templars; the chief and hieroglyphic number of the Freemasons is three times three. The Templars held Divine Service in places which were interdicted. By the strictest observances they reserved these for themselves (or set these aside) they appealed to the rights of their forefathers.

In the general organization, Roessler tells us:

The Brother Templars were, according to their statutes as Hospital Brothers divided into three classes: 1, into the class of the serving who, without distinction, nursed sick pilgrims and Knights Templars; 2, into that of the spiritual Brothers destined for the service of pilgrims; 3, into that of Knights who went to war.

We find in the Instructions of the Chevalier d'Orient where are celebrated the foundation of the Knights Templars and the spread of their teachings in Europe the following declaration on the matter is given:

"Eighty-one Masons* under the leadership of Garimonts, the Patriarch of Jerusalem, went, in the year 1150, to Europe and betook themselves to the Bishop of Upsala who received them in very friendly fashion and was consequently initiated into the mysteries of the Copts which the Masons had brought with them; later he was entrusted with the deposit of the collection of those teachings, rites and mysteries. The Bishop took pains to enclose and conceal them in the subterranean vaults of the tower of the 'Four Crowns' which at that time, was the crown treasure chamber of the King of Sweden. Nine of these Masons, amongst them Hugo de Paganis, founded in Europe the Order of the Knights Templars; later on they received from the Bishop the dogmas, mysteries and teachings of the Coptic Priests, confided to him.

"Thus in a short time the Knights Templars became the receivers and depositors of the mysteries, rites and

---

* "These Masons are always in the figurative sense Knights of the Cross who had been admitted to the mysteries of the working in the mystic Temple, and to the religion of the Children of the Widow."

THE TEMPLARS.   95

ceremonies which had been brought over by the Masons from the East—the Levites of the *true Light*.

"The Knights Templars, devoted entirely to the sciences and to the dogmas brought from the Thebaid, wished, in course of time, to preserve this doctrine in solemn fashion by a token. The Scotch Templars served as pattern in the matter, they having founded the three degrees of St. Andreas of Scotland, and adapted them to the allegorical legend to be found in the instructions referred to.

"Scotch Templars were occupied in excavating a place at Jerusalem in order to build a temple there, and precisely on the spot where the temple of Solomon—or at least that part of it called the Holy of Holies—had stood. During their work they found three stones which were the corner stones of the Solomon temple itself. The monumental form of these excited their attention; this excitement became all the more intense when they found the name Jehovah engraved in the elliptical spaces of the last of these stones— this which was also a type of the mysteries of the Copt—the sacred word which, by the murder of the Master Builder, had been lost, and which, according to the legend of the first degree, Hiram had had engraved on the foundation stone of Solomon's temple. After such a discovery the Scotch Knights took this costly memorial with them, and, in order eternally to preserve their esteem for it, they employed these as the three corner stones of their first temple at Edinburgh."*

Our author further tells us that:

The works began on St. Andreas' day; and so the Templars who had knowledge of this fact, of the secret of the three stones, and of the re-discovered word, called them-

---

* The legend of these three stones has a striking resemblance to that of the three mysterious stones which the Nymphs found and brought to Minerva—the Goddess of Wisdom.

selves Knights of St. Andreas ; they appointed degrees of merit in order to attain, and these are present in the apprentice, companion, and master degrees known under the name of the Little Master-Builder, the Great Master-Builder, and the Scotch Master.

By the instruction common to all Knightly Orders the Crusaders were under obligation to make many journeys and pilgrimages where, as is said, they had to see themselves surrounded by dangers. Therefore they founded those degrees in order to recognize each other and to assist each other in need. For these journeys they took signs, words, and particular touches or grips, and imparted to all Brothers a principal sign in order to find help in case of a surprise.

In order to imitate the Christians of the East and the Coptic Priests, these Knights preserved among themselves the verbal law which was never written down, and took care that it should remain concealed to the initiated of the lower degrees. All this is preserved with exactitude in the philosophic rite of our days, although this rite does not precisely seek to derive its origin from the Knights Templars.

The Knights Templars united the possessions of the Old Man of the Mountains under their rule, as they had perceived the supernatural courage of his pupils, they admitted these into their order. Some historians have thus come to the opinion that the Knights Templars had been induced themselves to accept the institutions of those admitted. Gauthier von Montbar was acquainted with these teachings, and transplanted them into Europe.

All these circumstances were very detrimental to the religion of Rome ; it lost many of those who had belonged to it ; more especially many Crusaders who were sojourning in Syria, Palestine and Egypt, where all the forms of belief of the first Christians were preserved and tolerated by the Saracens.

Eastern Christians regarded the dogma of the unity of

God as a mystery and saw in it a divine manifestation. They, therefore, only imparted the knowledge thereof at initiation which they held very secret. They practised the morality commanded by the Son of Mary, but did not believe in his divinity; for all those who followed Gnostic and Kabalistic traditions considered him to be their Elder Brother.

The Knights of the Cross who had come to know these dogmas and mysteries of the Christians of the East, were obliged, when they had returned to Europe, to hold this initiation still more secret, for the mere suspicion of such a faith would have been sufficient to bring these new religious professors to the rack and the stake.*

We will now pass on to some of the religious and philosophic views held by the Knights Templars which are summarized from the Abbé Grégoire and which show the link with the Gnostic teachings.

The Order of the Temple is cosmopolitan; it is divided into two great classes: 1, the Order of the East; 2, the Order of the Temple.

The Order of the Temple sprang from the Order of the East, of which ancient Egypt was the cradle. The Order of the East comprised different orders or classes of adepts. The adepts of the first order were at once legislators, judges, and pontiffs.

Their policy was opposed to the propagation of metaphysical knowledge and the natural sciences, of which they made themselves the sole depositories; and whoever should have dared to reveal the secrets reserved for the initiates in the order of the sacerdotal hierarchy, would have been punished with most dire severity. They gave to the people only unintelligible emblems constituting the exoteric

---

* Accerrelos (Roessler, Dr. Karl), *History of Freemasonry*, Leipzig, 1836. II., p. 85 *et seq.*

theology, which was a compound of absurd dogmas and extravagant practices tending to give more ascendency to superstition, and to consolidate the government.

Moses was initiated in Egypt. He was profoundly versed in the theological, physical, and metaphysical mysteries of the priests. Aaron, his brother, and the other Hebrew chiefs became the depositories of these doctrines. These chiefs or Levites were divided into several classes, according to the custom of the Egyptian priests.

Later on, the Son of God was born into the world. He was brought up in the Alexandrian school. Filled with a spirit altogether divine, endowed with the most marvellous intelligence, he succeeded in attaining all the degrees of Egyptian initiation.

On returning to Jerusalem, he presented himself before the chiefs of the Synagogue, and pointed out to them the numerous alterations that the Law of Moses had undergone at the hands of the Levites; he confounded them by the power of his spirit and the extent of his knowledge; but the Jewish priests, blinded by their passions, persisted in their errors.

However, the moment had come when Jesus Christ, directing the fruit of his lofty meditations towards the universal civilization and welfare of the world, tore down the veil which hid the truth from the people, preached the love of one's neighbour and the equality of all men before the common Father. Finally, consecrating by a sacrifice worthy of the Son of God the heavenly doctrines which he had come to spread, he established for ever on the earth, by his gospels, the religion inscribed in the Book of Eternity.

Jesus conferred on his disciples the evangelical initiation, caused his spirit to descend upon them, divided them into different orders, according to the custom of the Egyptian priests and Hebrew priests, and placed them under the authority of St. John, his beloved disciple, and whom he had made supreme pontiff and patriarch.

John never quitted the East; his doctrine, always pure, was not altered by the admixture of any other doctrine.

Peter and the other apostles, on the contrary, carried the teachings of Jesus Christ to distant peoples; but as they were often forced, in order to propagate the faith, to conform to the manners and customs of these different nations, and even to admit other rites than those of the East, slight variations and changes crept into the different gospels, as well as into the doctrines of the numerous Christian sects.

Down to 1118, the mysteries and the hierarchical order of the Egyptian initiation, transmitted to the Jews through Moses and afterwards to the Christians through Jesus Christ, were religiously preserved by the successors of the apostle John. These mysteries and these initiations regenerated through the evangelical initiation or baptism formed a sacred deposit which, thanks to the simplicity of primitive customs from which the brothers of the East never departed, never underwent the slightest alteration.

The Christians of the East, persecuted by the infidels, appreciating the courage and piety of those valiant crusaders who, sword in one hand and cross in the other, flew to the defence of the holy places; doing justice, above all, to the virtues and the ardent charity of Hugh of Payens, considered it their duty to entrust to hands so pure the treasures of knowledge acquired during so many centuries, and sanctified by the cross, the teachings and the ethics of the Man-God.

Hugh was then invested with the patriarchal apostolic power, and placed in the legitimate line of the successors of John the Apostle or Evangelist.

Such is the origin of the foundation of the Templars, and of the introduction amongst them of the different modes of initiation of the Christians of the East designated by the name of Primitive or Johannite Christians. It is to this initiation that belong the various degrees consecrated by the rules of the Temple, and which were so much called in question in the famous but terrible action brought against this august Order.

Jacques de Molay, foreseeing the misfortunes that threatened the Order, appointed as his successor Brother Jean Marc Larmenius, of Jerusalem, whom he invested with full patriarchal apostolic authority, and with magisterial power.

This Grand Master passed on the supreme power to Brother Theobald, of Alexandria, as is evidenced by the charter of transmission, etc.

Let us come finally to the Levitical doctrines :—God is all that exists ; every part of all that exists is a part of God, but is not God.

Immutable in his essence, God is mutable in his parts, which after having existed under the laws of certain combinations more or less complex, live again under laws of fresh combinations. All is increate.

God being supremely intelligent, every one of the parts which compose him is endowed with a portion of his intelligence, in virtue of its destiny, whence it follows that there is an infinite gradation of intelligences resulting from an infinity of different compounds, the union of which forms the entirety of the worlds. This entirety is the Great All, or God, who alone has the power to modify, change, and govern all these orders of intelligences, according to the eternal and immutable laws of an infinite justice and goodness.

God—infinite Being—is composed of three powers ; the Father, or Being ; the Son, or action ; the Spirit, or mind, proceeding from the power of the Father and the Son. These three powers form a trinity, a power infinite, unique and individual.

There is but one only true religion, that which acknowledges one only God, Eternal, filling the infinity of time and space.

The Order of Nature is immutable; therefore all doctrines that any one would attempt to build up on a change of these laws would be founded only on error. . .

Eternal life is the power with which every being is endowed, of living in his own life and of acquiring an infinity of modifications by combining himself unceasingly with other beings, according to what is ordained by the eternal laws of the wisdom, the justice and the infinite goodness of the supreme Intelligence.

According to this system of modification of matter, it is natural to conclude that all its parts have the right of thought and free-will, and therefore the power of merit and demerit; hence there is no longer anything of what is called inorganic matter; if, however, any must be admitted, where is the limit, for instance, among mineral, vegetable, and animal substances?

However, the high Initiates do not profess to believe that all the parts of matter possess the faculty of thought. It is not thus that they profess to understand their system. They certainly admit a series of intelligences from the elementary substance, the most simple molecule, or the monad, up to the reunion of all these monads or of their compounds, a reunion which would constitute the great All, or God, which, as the Universal Intelligence, would alone have the power of comprehending Itself. But the manner of being, of feeling, and of using the intelligences, would be relative to the hierarchical order in which they found themselves placed; consequently the intelligence would differ according to the mode of organization and the hierarchical place of each body. Thus, according to this system, the intelligence of the simple molecule would be limited to seeking or rejecting union with certain other molecules. The intelligence of a body composed of several molecules would have other characters, according to the mode of organization of its elements, and the higher or lower degree that it occupied in the hierarchical scale of compounds. Man, for example, among the intelligences which form part of the earth, would alone have that modification or organization which would fully give the "I" consciousness, as well as the faculty of *distinguishing* good from evil, and consequently which would procure the gift of free-will.

Such is a summary of the version given by the Abbé Grégoire* of some of the inner philosophy held by the Knights Templars. There is a distinctly Eastern tone of thought in even these few fragments, fragments which indicate quite clearly to many students the sources from which these traditions were drawn.

The Strict Observance endeavoured to reconstitute a Gnostic teaching when it sought to revive the Traditions of the Templars.

---

* Grégoire (Abbé), *Histoire des Sectes Religieuses*, II., pp. 292 *et seq.* Paris, 1828.

THE TROUBADOURS,

The Singing Messengers from East to West.

> Oh, these are voices of the Past,
> Links of a broken chain.—Procter.

MYSTERIOUS songsters of the Middle Ages, messengers who were burdened—by right of the royal gift of song—with a knowledge that transcended that of their fellow-men—such were the Troubadours, who formed an integral portion of the mystic thread, and thus served in the weaving of the glorious traditions of eastern arcane lore into the young web of the western child-life.

Much has been already set down by many competent writers on this most complicated and interesting period of the Middle Ages; here and there some few frankly acknowledge that in the study of the writings and poems of the Troubadours, traces of hidden knowledge on their part become revealed, a knowledge which pertains to some more ancient tradition than that of the Catholic Church.

It is these traces that must be collected, in order to demonstrate that these "Messengers of Love," as they were often termed, were inheritors of a "Kingdom of Heaven"—a mystic heaven, indeed, of pure doctrine, noble life, and holy aspirations.

It is but slightly that we need touch on their general history, for the outer aspect of their work can be easily followed by students; our chief attention must be centred on the most important part of their mission, and the part but little known in the general world, namely, that of their work as spiritual teachers, their secret language, and above all their secret doctrine.

Rossetti* in his valuable book gives many proofs of the existence of a mystic language in the "Secret Schools," and of the "double" and even "triple language" used by these Troubadours in communicating with each other. These details must be investigated if we desire to arrive at any clear comprehension of the extent to which these Secret Schools were organized and developed during the Middle Ages, and on this point Rossetti writes as follows:

> The existence of such a style of language is an historical fact affirmed by many, and denied by none; it is a not less notorious fact that the persecuted sect conformed in public to the language and ceremonies of the persecuting religion; while they give in secret to every

---

* Rossetti (Gabriele), *Disquisitions on the Anti-papal Spirit which produced the Reformation*, ii, 112, 170. London, 1834.

sentence of that language, and to every act of those ceremonies, an arbitrary and conventional meaning, corresponding with their own designs. There is scarcely a contemporary or succeeding historian who does not tell us that the Patarini, or Cathari, or Albigenses, were Manicheans; and we know that Silvanus, one of the successors of the murdered Manes, so artfully used that doctrine "that it seemed all drawn from the Scriptures, as they are received by catholics. He affected to make use of Scriptural phrases and he spoke like the most orthodox among us, when he mentioned the baptism, death, burial or resurrection of our Lord Jesus Christ." And he and his proselytes did all this so cunningly that "the Manicheans seduced numbers of people; and their sect was considered by the simple-minded to be a society of Christians, who made profession of an extraordinary perfection." These are the words of the Abbé Pluquet (*Dict. des Hérés.*, art., Silvan and Manicheans), who traced the existence of this sect in Italy as far back as 1022, when many of them were discovered and burned for the love of God. Let us hear the same author describe the actions of later sectarians after other innumerable examples of inhuman cruelty. "The *Clanculars* were a society of anabaptists who taught that *on religious subjects* it was necessary to speak *in public like other men*, and only *in secret* to express the thoughts." And the Albigensis and Manicheans show the best means of succeeding in this design with the following fact.

Persecuted incessantly by the remorseless Inquisition, one of their chiefs had recourse to a cunning device. He knew that he and his friends were accused of refusing to worship the saints, and of denying the supremacy of the Romish Church, and that they would be forced to make a profession of faith and to swear by the *Holy Mary* to have no other religion than that of the *Holy Church*. He was resolved not to betray his inward sentiments, but he desired if possible, to escape *death*. "O, muses! O, high genius!

Now vouchsafe your aid!" He shut himself up in a cave with two aged females of his own sect, and gave the name of *Holy Church* to the one and *Holy Mary* to the other, "In order, that, when the sectarians were interrogated by the Father Inquisitors, they might be able to swear by the *Holy Mary* that they held no other faith than that of the *Holy Church*." Hence, when we desire to estimate properly the devout and holy things written in those times, we must first consider who composed them; and thus we shall be able to reconcile the frequent contradictions which are apparent between the verses and the actions of the Troubadours and Trouveurs."*

It is remarkable that this secret language should have remained so little known, since it gives a clue of almost unmeasured importance to many a hidden mystery in the Troubadour life of the Middle Ages. It is to Eugène Aroux that we owe the largest debt of gratitude for unveiling this mysterious bye-way of mystic studies; he denounces, with the wrath

---

* Rossetti, Gabriele, *Disquisitions on the Antipapal Spirit which produced the Reformation*, ii., 113-115. London, 1834.

Another writer makes the following comment:—"D'après les idées de M. Rossetti, il y aurait encore dans les poésies de Dante et de Pétrarque, ainsi que dans les romans de Boccace, quelque chose que ces hommes n'ont jamais entièrement exprimé dans leurs écrits latins. Il semblerait, à entendre le nouveau commentateur de la Divine Comédie, qu'une grande et éternelle vérité, partie de la bouche des Orphées, des Thalés, des Pythagores, et bondissant d'écho en écho jusqu'a nous, par l'intermédaire des prophètes, de Platon, des Sibylles, de Virgile et de Boétius, a été recueillie enfin, tenue voilée, mais exactement transmise aux générations modernes, par une succession de sectaires, comme les manichéens, les templiers, les patarins, les gibelins, les rosecroix, les sociniens, les swedenborgiens, les francs-maçons, et enfin les carbonari."
—Delécluze (E. J.), *Dante Alighieri, ou la Poésie Amoureuse;* pp. 605-606. Paris, 1848.

of a good, but bigoted Catholic, the teachings of Dante, and he unveils for us the real reason of his wrath: and from his standpoint he is right, Dante was not an orthodox Catholic; he was a true mystic, and his church was composed of all those great and liberated souls who have existed in every clime: without distinction of race, religion or caste. Aroux draws the attention of the student to the following important points: with relation to the real views of Dante, thus he says, in commenting on the poet:

Though we may seem to have gone back quite beyond the deluge, it is evident that we are really completely in the Middle Ages. And in fact, though people may talk to us of the origin of the human species and of its dispersion over the earth, the question is really that of the starting-point of the Manichean-Gnostic doctrine and of its course from East to West. Let the following lines be carefully considered: " We do not readily believe that men were, immediately on the confusion of tongues, dispersed all over the world. The root of the human race was first planted *in the countries of the East*, then OUR RACE spread itself *by putting forth* numerous *shoots on one side and another*, [like] PALM-TREES, and it finally reached the *extreme boundaries of the West*, whence it resulted that *rational throats* quenched their thirst for the first time at the streams of Europe, at some at least, if not at all. But whether they were *foreigners* coming there for the first time, or whether, *born in Europe*, they had returned there, they brought with them a *triple* language."

Here is the text of this passage, so singular as it is, understood in a literal sense:

"*Ex præcedenti memorata confusione linguarum non leviter opinamur per universa mundi climata . . . tunc homines primum fuisse dispersos. Et cum radix humanæ propaginis principaliter in oris orientalibus sit plantata; nec non ab inde ad utrumque per diffusos multipliciter* PALMITES. NOSTRA *fuit extensa* PROPAGO; *demumque ad fines occidentales protracta, unde primitus tunc vel totius Europæ, vel saltem quædam,* RATIONALIA GUTTURA *potaverunt. Sed sive* ADVENÆ *tunc* PRIMITUS ADVENISSENT, *sive ad Europam* INDIGENÆ REPETISSENT, *idioma secum* TRIFARIUM *homines attulerunt."*

However little it may now be remembered that, according to Dante, those only are men who make use of their reason, others being brutes in his eyes; that, further, he has taken care to explain to us in the *Vita Nuova* that the name of palms, *palmieri*, was affected by those who had made the pilgrimage to Jerusalem, it will be acknowledged that the true meaning of this passage is quite different from that which we have given it, and that it conceals another which is as follows:

Our doctrine had its origin in the East; its votaries, constituting the true human race, were not at first spread all over the earth: it was by slow degrees that our Sectarian race, *nostra propago*, multiplied itself with the help of Syrian pilgrims, *palms palmieri*, who brought the light to the confines of the West, and then rational throats, men using their reason, quenched their thirst at the streams of Europe. These missionaries of the sect being either Orientals or Europeans returning to the country of their birth, they brought with them a language of threefold meaning, allegorical, moral, and mystical.

To reject an interpretation so plain and so thoroughly in accordance with all that we have previously seen, it would have to be explained how it could have come into Dante's head that men were born in Europe, when no rational throat had as yet drunk of its streams, that these Europeans had been to the East to learn a triple language, to bring it back into their own country, which no doubt had one of its own, and that the human race born in the East had to people the West, already inhabited by men, whether rational or not. Now this explanation is none of the easiest.

It is always the case that these importers of the *triple language* are divided into three bands, having each their own idiom; to one was allotted the south of Europe, to another the north, to the third the part of Asia and of Europe occupied by those who are now called Greeks, *quos nunc Græcos vocamus*, as if they did not bear this name ages ago. But let us explain: here it is a question of the refugees of the sect, of the Sinon of the party, whom we have seen so ill-treated in hell, who are also spoken of in the *Monarchy* under the name of *Greek pastors*. These hold to white and yellow, as one of the aspects of Lucifer; they have one foot on the European soil of the Catholics, the other on the eastern land of the Manicheans, and, which is very disturbing, they understand for the most part the artifices of the conventional vocabulary. The three idioms were then subdivided in each of the regions mentioned; but those of the north, such as the Hungarians, Slavs, Teutons, Saxons, and English kept the monosyllable *is* as the sign of their common origin. For the rest of Europe there was a third idiom, "though *it may not be perceived* that it is triple, *licet nec videatur trifarium.*" Among the inhabitants of this region, "some say, as affirmation, *oc*, others *oil*, and others again *si*; that is to say, Spaniards, French, and Italians. But what proves the common origin of their idiom is that they use some of the same words to express many things, such as *Dieu, ciel, amour, mer, terre, vivre, mourir, aimer, and others besides.* [*God, heaven, love, sea, earth, to live, to die, to love.*]"

Dante knew very well that the Spaniards did not use *oc* as an affirmation, that they used *si* like the Italians, but he desired to call attention to the chief centre of the Albigensian doctrine, to the land of the langue d'oc, and not venturing to name Toulouse, he made use of this very visible artifice, especially when it is recognized that the words which he mentions as revealing the common origin of the language in the three countries are precisely those which the sectarian poets so frequently use in their mysterious compositions.

Aroux further explains that these " importers " of the " triple language " were divided into three bands, each having its own idiom: one set traversed the south of Europe, another the north, another the part of Asia and Europe occupied by those now called Greeks. Then Aroux breaks out in wrath: "They have one foot on the European soil of the Catholics, the other on the eastern land of the Manichæans."

But it is from another of his interesting works† that we get the most intimate details about the organization of these Troubadour heretics, and their spiritual teaching; the passages are so important that it is better to give them in full.‡

The eminent professor§ whom we follow untiringly because he is an authority on the subject, had no suspicion, when making researches into the elements composing the

---

* Aroux (Eugène), *Dante Hérétique, Révolutionnaire et Socialiste, Révélations d'un Catholique*, p. 388. Paris, 1854.

† Aroux (E.), *Les Mystères de la Chevalerie*, pp. 161-169. Paris, 1858.

‡ The phrases "True human race" and "Sectarians" are generally applied to Mystics, also to the Manichæans, Albigenses, Troubadours, Palmers, and Palmieri ; it meant those men and women throughout the world, of every nation and in every clime, who were seeking the inner life in its true sense ; and who will be the "first fruits" of the "Redeemer," in the mystical sense.

§ Aroux is here referring to Fauriel (M.P., Paris), whose works on the Provençal literature have been so often quoted in these pages.

personnel of Provençal literature, that he was digging into the archives of the Albigensian Church. So it is, however, as will be shown by a rapid estimate of these elements in the light of common sense. One may believe with him that previous to the XIth century there were in the south of France men, who under the name of jesters, *joculatores*, made it their profession to recite or to sing romantic fictions. But it was precisely because the apostles of the dissenting doctrine found this custom established in the countries where it had survived the Roman domination, that they eagerly adopted it for the furtherance of their propaganda. For just as they excelled in turning to account the heroic traditions, the religious fables of the various peoples in order to engraft their ideas on this national foundation, they displayed exceeding skill in adapting themselves, according to times and places, to the manners and customs of the countries in which they carried on their ministry. Thus they became *minnesingers* in Germany, bards and skalds in Scandinavia, minstrels in England, *trouvères* in northern France, troubadours and jugglers in ancient Aquitaine, *giullari*, men of mirth, in Italy—leaving everywhere monuments of their genius and a most popular memory.

The missionaries of the heresy certainly preached the religion of love long before the time when William of Poitiers spoke of them, towards 1100, by the name of Troubadours, for before winning over the higher classes of society, their doctrines must have taken a long time to filter through the lower ranks.

At the time of the complete organization* of the sectarian propaganda, that is to say from 1150 to 1200, the most brilliant period of Provençal literature, Fauriel rightly distinguishes different orders of troubadours and jesters,

---

* This was just before the most deadly persecutions began. There was an extraordinarily extended organization of this so-called heretical church.

the very necessity of things having obliged their division into two distinct classes. The one in fact addressing themselves more especially to social parties, singing only for courts and castles; the other, appealing more to popular instincts, composed for public places, for the mercantile and working classes, for the country population. We have said that the former were the dissenting bishops, combining the qualities of the Perfect Knights and the Perfect Troubadours. We have explained how, having no less courage than skill, knowing how at need to employ cunning, and giving constant evidence of a patience and humility proof against everything, they were of the type of Renaud de Montauban, the chivalrous figure in contrast to Maître Renard, the symbolical representative of the Roman clergy.

The latter, no less useful on account of the recruits that they unceasingly made amongst the most numerous classes, amongst those who had most to suffer from clerical oppression and exactions, furnished the model of the knights errant, as also that of the wild knights ["*chevaliers sauvages*"], personified in the romance of which Guido the Wild is the easily to be recognized hero.

Lastly, above these two orders of knights and troubadours, there was that of the barons and feudal lords, who, having embraced the Albigensian faith, having become its protectors or godfathers, carried on the propaganda in their own way and in their own social sphere. These men often cultivated poetry, and used it to impress on the nobility, and still more on the *bourgeoisie*, ideas hostile to pontifical omnipotence. Not only did they encourage the people to shake off the theocratic yoke by setting them the example, but they further upheld them and resolutely took up their defence against prelates, inquisitors and legates, the Estults, Galaffrons, giants and necromancers that abound in the romances of Geste. Thence, we have that heroic personage Roland, in contrast to Master Issengrin; that son of Milo, whose powerful words, under the name of Durendal, made

THE TROUBADOURS. 113

an enormous breach in the granite of the mountains, a breach through which an invasion was made on to Spanish soil, where it could exclaim, long before Louis XIV., "The Pyrenees exist no longer!"

These noble sectaries, of the type of the chivalric Roland, were, as a matter of fact, feudal lords, true knights. As such, they did not hesitate to confer in case of need, in accordance with the ideas of the time, and especially in masonic [? "*masseniques*"] lodges, the order of knighthood on distinguished members of their communion whom religious or political interest drew into foreign countries.

On another side, observe how generously certain German Emperors—such as a Conrad, an Otho, the two Fredericks—once came down into Italy, lent themselves to bestowing the order of knighthood on the bourgeois of Milan, on merchants and bankers of Genoa and Florence. For them it was a means of recruiting their forces against the papacy, and of strengthening in Italy an opposition which they well knew to be not simply political. And Dante also is careful not to forget the families who quartered on their shields "the arms of the great baron," vicar of the Emperor Otho; and it is with pride that he recalls the promotion of his great-great-grandfather Cacciaguida, knighted by Conrad.

As to the jesters, properly so-named jesters of song, of sayings, of romance, as they were called—they must be distinguished from the *mimic* jesters, that is to say, from the mountebanks and buffoons. The clerical jesters were, as has already been said, evangelical ministers, still subject to the preliminary discipline of the priesthood. Holding the rank of deacons in the sectarian church, they were with regard to the pastors to whom they were attached, in a position analogous to that of squires to knights, and it is under this title that they figure in the romances.

If distinguished troubadours are spoken of, and, among others, Giraud de Borneil, as always accompanied by two jesters, it is unquestionably that these troubadours were *Albigensian bishops*, whose dignity and functions required the assistance of two deacons. This is why it is said of them that "*They never went on a tour* (episcopal) without having both of them in their retinue."

It would be a great mistake to think that the first comer could be admitted to the functions of a jester. Fauriel will tell you that it was necessary to have "an extraordinary memory, a fine voice, to be able to sing well, to play well on the accompanying instrument, and also to have a knowledge of history, of traditions, of genealogies. Several jesters indeed are cited for their historical knowledge." The learned member of the Institute thinks that this knowledge could not have been very great, at a time when all history was reduced to barren chronicles; but is it quite certain that their blunders, their anachronisms, their confounding of personages, countries, and dates, may not be voluntary? Would they not on the contrary be a proof that their knowledge in this respect was much greater than one is willing to suppose? As to the genealogies, it is a question of those of Geste's romances.

Besides the jesters attached to the person of the bishop or of the mere pastor, were those who, having already completed their probation, went forth, furnished with the recommendation of the one or the other, to give instruction or carry consolation into courts and castles. It was these who were called *elder sons* [of age? "*fils majeurs*"], deacons of the first-class. The others, designated *younger sons* [under age? "*fils mineurs*"], performed the same functions in towns and villages; but for the most part their own special aptitudes marked them out for the kind of service expected from them.

These two classes of one and the same priesthood were recruited from all ranks of society, on the sole condition of uniting to a true vocation the natural gifts and the knowledge necessary for success in so difficult and dangerous a mission.

One curious matter, to state precisely, would be how many personages came *down* into these poetic classes from a station generally considered superior. Nothing was more common in the 12th and 13th centuries, in the countries of the Provençal tongue, than to see knights, castellans, canons, clerics, become troubadours or simple jesters. Several of the most distinguished among both had begun by being considerable personages in society. Peyrols had been a knight; Pierre Cardinal was born of a noble and wealthy family; Pierre Roger had been a canon at Clermont; Arnaud de Marueilh had been a clergyman, and the famous Arnaud Daniel was a noble who had received a first-rate education. Assuredly these men did not consider that they were lowering themselves by embracing the apostolate, but on the contrary were raising themselves in their own eyes and in those of their brethren. The mysterious Sordello was a noble lord.

Moreover, how should knights such as Sordello, such as the Dauphin of Auvergne and so many others, have hesitated to become troubadours out of zeal for their faith, when kings like Richard of England and Peter of Aragon, powerful suzerains like William of Poitiers, had declared themselves professors of the Gay Science; when they added their voices to those of the servants of love, to exalt, in interests perhaps less religious than political, the mysterious and Perfect lady who under various names—as star, flower, light—was appealed to, to cast down to hell the Roman she-wolf, to crush the pontifical serpent? The *Infamous* dates not from Voltaire.

Just as episcopal mandates, days for the sermons of preachers, and the order of the offices, &c., are affixed to the doors of churches, so did the troubadours give out their notices in the castles by a kind of poetical programme, thus making known the lyric, pastoral or romantic compositions which were to serve as the text for their teachings. In how many places was not the Divine Comedy thus recited and commented on before a select audience? Fauriel cites as a specimen a whimsical piece by Pierre Cardinal, "in which the author," he says, "envelops himself in veils of allegory of the most fantastic kind till it appears to him unintelligible." These veils would have appeared to him transparent if he had understood the true composition of the balsam of Fierabras.

As this famous balsam, the unguent proclaimed by the troubadour knight and probably bishop, Pierre Cardinal, the unguent which *heals all kinds of wounds*, even the bites *of the venemous reptiles* (in the orthodox ranks, be it understood)—is in fact none other than the word of the Gospel; so also the *golden vessel* in which it is contained, the vessel adorned with the most precious stones, is none other than the *Holy Grail itself, or the book of the Gospels, as the Albigenses had adopted and translated it; the golden book, the vessel containing the true light, visible only to the initiated, to the professors of the gay science* ["*du gay saber*"]. Now, among the romances given out by Pierre Cardinal, we find in the nick of time that of Tristan of Léonois, so well-known to Dante, and which, celebrating the conquest of England by the law of love, should have more than one claim to the interest of the people of Provence.

We have seen, on the one hand, that the Albigensian clergy, so skilful and so full of zeal, were recruited from the ranks of the priesthood as well as from those of the nobility and the bourgeoisie; on the other hand we have become convinced, from the interpretations that we have given of the decrees of the Courts of Love and of the decisions in the amorous casuistry, that ecclesiastics converted to the faith of Love could not continue their cure of souls in the parish where they had performed their vicarial functions.

What then became of those fresh recruits enrolled under

the banner of heresy when once dispossessed of their cure or of any other sacerdotal function?

Like the other aspirants to the sectarian priesthood, they went into seminaries or lodges to receive instruction; then, having become deacons or squires, having undergone tests and given the required pledges, they were admitted to the rank of Perfect Knights, or Perfect Troubadours. Having thus graduated, they started in the character of missionaries or of *pilgrims of love* ("pellegrini d'amore") as Dante says, sometimes undertaking long and dangerous journeys. And so we find traces of them everywhere, from the icy north and the depths of Germany even to the east, in France and the low countries, in England, Spain and Italy. Then it was that, in the symbolical language of the faithful in love, they were called by the name of Knights-errant.

Preaching the doctrine of love, the true law of the Redeemer, their mission was to redress the wrongs of Rome, to take up the defence of the weak and oppressed; they were also represented and celebrated as the true soldiers of the Christ, the champions of the poor, attacking under all their forms the monstrous abuses of theocratic regime; as comforters of the *widow* Rachel, that Gnostic church so cruelly tried by the pontifical Herod; as the devoted supporters of the *sons of the widow*, those humble members of the "massenie" of the Holy Grail; as the terror of ogres, dragons, and giants.

Fauriel must then believe in them, writing: "It is unquestionable that in all the countries in Europe in which there were Knights, there was one particular class known by the title of *Knights errant;*" and he cites in proof of this the tax which was levied upon them in 1241 by Henry III. of England, who was in great need of money and would naturally turn to his best allies to obtain it; would he necessarily call them by their true name of Albigensian missionaries?

"It is in the poetical monuments of southern France, he adds, that I find the most ancient traces of knight-errantry. What may be gathered from them as a whole, is that the condition of Knight errant was rather *accidental* and *transitory* than fixed and permanent." Where else indeed than in Provence could one find more traces of their pilgrims of love since Provence was their native soil? And was it not the least that could be expected, after the trials of a wandering life, that these zealous missionaries, called back to sedentary functions, might rest after their prolonged fatigue?

Contrary to the romances which represent them as always solitary, and running about in search of adventures, "the Provençal poets depict them to us as usually travelling several together, and to all appearance temporarily associated for some enterprise or common *quest*." Yes, indeed! Exactly like the missionaries of our own times, and they were always accompanied by their *socius*, whom the Troubadours, their colleagues, turned into their squire.

One of the most illustrious among these knights-errant —an authentic personage, at least as a Troubadour—was Raimbaud de Vaqueiras, whose platonic *amours* with Madame Beatrice, who called him her *beautiful knight* ("beau chevalier"), are extremely curious, but would make too long an episode. We will merely say that Boniface, Marquis de Montferrat, whose sister Raimbaud's Beatrice must have been, was one of the nobles of the south of Europe who most especially occupied the attention of the Troubadours, for the very simple reason that, sharing their faith, he sheltered under his protection the Vaudois, whose cradle was in the valleys of Piedmont.

Other knights are mentioned at the same period in the historical monuments of the south of France and of the Catalogue, under the name of the "*Chevalier Sauvages*"— *Wild Knights*. The romance entitled "Guido, the Wild," presents the poetical personification of these *guides* or pastors of Alpine districts. He figures in Ariosto's "Roland," which we shall probably annotate some day, with some heroes whose symbolical value is not more difficult to estimate.

An article of certain constitutions of James I., of Aragon, who wanted to treat with Rome, forbade in 1234, the making of Wild Knights; another article, says Fauriel, "seems to establish a connection between this class of Knights and the jesters; it prohibits the giving of any gratuities to a *jester* or to a *Wild Knight*." I can well believe it, and such a connection was a matter of course. Was not the jester the squire, the *socius* of the Wild Knight, and the King of Aragon wishing to give pledges to Rome, how could he separate them in the prohibition he was issuing? Would not the gratuity given to one have been given to the other? The Wild Knights had in reality the closest relations with the Knights errant; like them they were ministers of the proscribed worship, forced to disguise their character carefully. They differed from them on one point only, and that was that instead of going to a foreign land to catechise and convert the orthodox population, they had to fulfil their own ministry in their own native country. Further, instead of exercising sedentary functions in a single parish, they had to move over a much more extensive area. They were obliged to go up hill and down dale, in Alpine districts, to carry the words of peace and *consolation* to the isolated populations, who were too few in number to have a resident pastor; and also to those whom persecution or the stake had deprived of their own.

Unlike the ministers of towns, boroughs and castles, the *gentle* knights, as titularies of this or that church, their *lady-love*—they themselves were the pastors of the woods and mountains, compelled, in order to feed their sheep, to travel through the wildest districts; hence the name given to them by their co-religionists, who caused it to be taken, like so many other conventional terms, outside their church, in a totally different sense.

The most bitter feeling on the part of the Catholics was aroused from the fact that the teachings they denounced were so closely allied to those inculcated by themselves, and that the lives of the heretics shone out as stars against the blackness of the mediæval monastic life.* Indeed, the majority of the higher classes became Troubadours, and when prevented by persecution from speaking, they took refuge in song,† and treated their subjects sometimes seriously, sometimes lightly, but ever was there, as we have seen, a dual meaning in *La gaie saber*, or the "Art of loving": for the true "union of love," as Aroux points out, meant the attachment of the "Perfect Chevalier" to the "celestial chivalry," for such were those knights‡ called who gave themselves to the service of the "Holy Grail," or the "Mystic Quest," *i.e.*, to the inner service, or initiation, of their secret body. They were indeed :

> The soldier-saints who, row on row,
> Burn upward each to his point of bliss.

The perfect passion of self-sacrifice was theirs, and moved those men of the Middle Ages to martyrdom and suffering in their zeal for the spreading of the knowledge of the mystic doctrine. Such, for

---

* Lecky (W. E. H., M.A.), *History of European Morals*, ii. 217. London, 1877.

† Thus we have the "Bible" of Guiot von Provins ; and the whole cycle of the "Grail legends."

‡ Wolfram von Eschenbach was one of these.

instance, was Peter Waldo,* who became the founder of the powerful groups of Waldensians,† or the "Poor of Lyons," a secret body with masonic connections. He was first attracted to serious subjects by a Troubadour who was reciting a poem in the streets of Lyons—a chant in favour of the ascetic life ; Waldo invited the Troubadour in, and from that time became one of them.

We must here digress from the mystic aspect, in order to give a slight outline on the general organisation, which can be taken from Baret's admirable work on the subject ;‡ he gives a chart of the chief School of Troubadours as follows : §

The School of Aquitaine
The School of Auvergne
The School of Rodez — All these were again sub-divided into groups.
The School of Languedoc
The School of Provence

The general compositions of the Troubadours may be classified under the following heads :

" The Gallant," " The Historical," " The Didactic," " The Satirical," and the purely " Theological " ; then

---

* See Gilly, D.D. (W. S.), *The Romaunt version of the Gospel according to St. John ;* from MSS. preserved in Trinity College, Dublin. Introduction, pp. xc. xcix.

† Also called Valdès, Valdernis, Valdensis, and then Waldensis.

‡ Baret (Eugène), *Les Troubadours et leur Influence sur la Littérature du Midi de l'Europe*, p. 64. Paris, 1867.

§ These are the French Schools only ; Germany, Italy, Austria, and the Danubian Provinces contained as many.

further, others we may term "The Mystical," or even "Hermetic"; the "Satirical" were often theological from an essentially belligerent standpoint. Baret emphasizes the fact that theological matters occupied the attention of the Troubadours much more than history. Nostradamus enumerates several works of this kind.* In the Vatican Library, says Baret, there are four anonymous treatises which belong to the Provençal literature.

But the object which was the special search of the Inquisition was the translation of the Bible into the Catalonian tongue, and very carefully was this work concealed; for the organization of these mystic schools was admirable and their bishops and deacons were disguised as Troubadours. Throughout Spain, Germany, Italy and Central Europe, this powerful "secret organization" extended with its mystic traditions. Aroux, in connecting the Troubadours with the Albigenses on one side, links them also to the Manichæan religion on the other, that most pernicious—according to the Roman Church—of all heresies, because the most vital; † and, indeed, nothing but the wholesale bloodshed undertaken by

---

* There is one of importance, *Traité sur la Doctrine des Albigeois et Tuschius*, by Raoul de Gassin.

† Says Lea: "When to Dualism is added the doctrine of transmigration as a means of reward and retribution, the sufferings of man seem to be fully accounted for. . . . Manes had so skilfully compounded Mazdean Dualism with Christianity and with Gnostic and Buddhist elements, that his doctrines found favour with high and low, with the subtle intellects of the Schools, and with the toiling masses." *Hist. of the Inquisition*, i. 89. London, 1888.

the Dominicans could have crushed out its public organization; still, it lived again in other forms and under other names, and when Rutherford and other writers connect the Manichæans with the Freemasons they are touching a deeper truth than perhaps they know. As the above-mentioned writer points out, the Troubadours and the "Steinmetzen or Bridge-Builders" were connected, and "among them, too, the Freemasons found ample occupation"; this is accurately true, for from Manes* "the widow's son," descends the tradition which was common to Troubadour and Freemason; their hieroglyphs were in many cases identical and the signs common to both. Manes went into Egypt and brought back from thence the ancient tradition, he who was crucified for reforming the Magian priesthood, became the originator of the powerful symbolic phrase used among "the sons of the widow" with its corresponding sign. It is this tradition which underlies the well-known societies of the Knight Templars, the Fratres Lucis, the Asiatische Brüder, and many others who have kept alive the mystic teaching, and handed it on.

From the death of Manes, 276 A.D., there was

---

* Mani—or Cubricus—was the pupil of Terebinthe (who was afterwards called Buddas). He was an Egyptian Philosopher, and from him Manes received the Hermetic tradition; Manichæism was based on the Ancient Babylonian religion with Christian, Persian and Egyptian elements introduced. The Gnostics who joined the Manichæan stream were the Basilideans, Marcionites, and Bardesanites. See Beausobre (M. de), *Histoire critique de Manichée*, 2 vols. Amsterdam, 1734.

an intimate alliance*—even a fusion—with some of the leading Gnostic sects, and thence do we derive the intermingling of the two richest streams of oriental Wisdom: the one, directly through Persia from India; the other, traversing that marvellous Egyptian period, enriched by the wisdom of the great Hermetic teachers, flowed into Syria and Arabia, and thence with added force—garnered from the new divine powers made manifest in the profound mystery of the blessed Jesus—into Europe, through Northern Africa, finding a home in Spain, where it took deep root. From this stock sprang into full flower that richness of speech and song for which the Troubadours will live for ever, Manichæans, who sang and chanted the Esoteric Wisdom they dared not speak.

Next we see them dispersed in sects, taking local names—separated in name only, but using the same secret language, having the same signs. Thus, everywhere they journeyed, and, no matter by what name they were called, each knew the other as a "widow's son," bound together on a Mystic Quest, knitted—by virtue of a secret science—into one community; with them came from the East the chivalric ideal, and they

---

* Says Lea: "Of all the heresies with which the early Church had to contend, none had excited such mingled fear and loathing as Manichæism." And again: "The Manichæism of the Cathari, Patarins, or Albigenses, was not a mere speculative dogma of the schools, but a faith which aroused fanaticism so enthusiastic that its devotees shrank from no sacrifices in its propagation." Lea (H. C.), *op. cit*, i. 89.

chanted of love and sang of heaven : but the love was a " Divine Love," and their heaven was the wisdom and peace of those who sought the higher life. As Aroux* says, the chief object which dominated the work of these " Trouveurs " [Troubadours] was chivalry — " not the feudal, fighting, iniquitous chivalry, as corrupt as it was ignorant," but that tone of thought which is well termed mystic, and which sees in all life only a manifestation of the Divine power ; they fought for the purity of their ideal against the ever-increasing corruption of the Roman Church.

A word must here be added on the origin of chivalry which is mistakenly supposed to be of Christian inception. Viardot says :

In recalling what Christian Europe owes to the Arabs with regard to knowledge, we must not omit what she owes to them with regard to manners. The high civilization to which they had attained bore its natural fruit, and the Arabs were no less distinguished by the advance and the gentleness of their manners than by the extent and variety of their knowledge. The humanity, the tolerance that they displayed towards conquered nations, to whom they generously left their possessions, their religion, their laws, and mostly their civic rights, bore a striking testimony on this point, which was thoroughly confirmed by their whole

---

* Aroux (Eugène), *Les Mystères de la Chevalerie*, pp. 69-71. aris, 1858.

"*Every Knight has the power to create Knights.* There is in the hand and in the sword of every Knight a power (I nearly wrote 'a fluid,' but I did not dare) which is really capable of creating other Knights."—Gautier (Léon), *Chivalry*, trs. Henry Frith, p. 223. London, 1891.

history. This high civilisation appeared under two chief aspects—gallantry in private manners, chivalry in public manners. Gallantry (as we will call the delicacy of social relations) arose among them from the extreme reserve imposed on the two sexes, from the severity of the laws and of opinion, in fine, from the cultivated mind of the women, who knew how to inspire love and to command respect. In all social relations, in all family customs, the Arabs showed extreme austerity. "Those people," they said of the Spaniards, "are full of courage, and endure privations with fortitude; but they live like wild beasts, washing neither their bodies nor even their clothes, which they only take off when they fall into rags, and *going into each other's houses without asking permission.*"*

Chivalry was the virtue of warriors. Founded on justice, it corrected the abuses of force, which is the right of war; founded on humanity, it tempered the excesses of hatred, reminding men of their brotherhood even in the midst of combat; it was a kind of association or confraternity between men of arms which drew together and united all its members when politics or religion separated them, and which imposed on them noble duties when all rights were disowned. Chivalry was the most powerful correction of feudalism by giving to the weak and the oppressed, protectors and avengers . . .

Bravery, however, the sole virtue of German soldiers, was neither the only one nor even the first, required of an Arab Knight. Ten qualities were indispensable to give him a right to this name, namely: goodness, valour, courtesy, poetry, elegance of speech, strength, horsemanship, skill in the use of lance, sword and bow.†

---

* "O believers! enter not into a strange house without asking permission to do so." (*Koran*, Sour. XXIV., v., 27). Jos. Conde, Part I., cap. 18.

† "Fue muy buen caballero, y se decia de él que tenia las diez prendas qué distinguen à los nobles y generosos, qué consisten en

This "Celestial Chivalry"—Aroux demonstrates—was derived from the "Albigensian Gospel," whose "Evangel" or "Gospel" was again derived from the Manichæan-Marcion tradition.* These Albigenses were identical with the Cathari, and the Troubadours were the links bearing the secret teaching from one body to another. "Thus one sees them taking every form: by turns, artizans, colporteurs, pilgrims, weavers, colliers . . . deprived of the right to speak, they took to singing."

It must be remembered that simultaneously with the inflow of this Manichæan Oriental wisdom into

---

bondad, valentia, caballeria, gentileza, poesia, bien hablar, fuerza, destreza en la lanza, en la espada, y en el tirar del arco." (J. Conde, perto II., cap. 63.)

He was an excellent Knight, and it was said of him that he possessed the ten accomplishments that distinguish nobles and honourable men, which consist in goodness, valour, horsemanship, courtesy, poetry, excellence of speech, ability, skill in lance, sword, and in drawing the bow.

The word "gentileza" or "gentillesse," which has greatly changed in meaning with the lapse of time, means charming manners, the good tone of a man well born and well bred, of one whom the English call a *gentleman*. Viardot (L), *Histoire des Arabes et des Mores d' Espagne*, ii., pp. 197, 199. Paris, 1851.

* Lea (H. C.), *op. cit.*, i. 92 : A further irrefragable evidence of the derivation of Catharism from Manichæism is furnished by the sacred thread and garment which were worn by all the Perfect among the Cathari. This custom is too peculiar to have had an independent origin, and is manifestly the Mazdean *kosti and saddarah*, the sacred thread and shirt, the wearing of which was essential to all believers, and the use of which, by both Zends and Brâhmins, shows that its origin is to be traced to the prehistoric period anterior to the separation of those branches of the Aryan family. Among the Cathari the wearer of the thread and vestment was what was known among the inquisitors as the '*hæreticus indutus*' or '*vestitus*,' initiated into all the mysteries of the heresy."

Spain, there had been the same development in Italy from Sicily, and all through the Danubian Provinces into Hungary, over the Caucasus to Russia, and along the shores of the Caspian Seas; just as the legend of the Holy Grail was everywhere, so also was this stream of thought, for the two were one.

The most prominent public development takes place, as we see, in the eleventh and twelfth centuries, but the enormous spread of the teaching was the result of centuries of quiet work. Travel was slow, and nearly all communication was from person to person. Hence when we see in the twelfth century the "flowering of the plant," it must be remembered that this result was the work in each country of small bands of—even isolated—travelling mystics who were true missionaries in life and heart.

To turn to another aspect it is curious to think of the Troubadours as authorities in dress and etiquette. Rutherford says: * " They prepared the youth of both sexes for society, and they drew up rules for their guidance therein," and then he gives a most interesting quotation from a Troubadour, Amanieu des Escas, who instructed a young man of rank while he was a Page or Esquire as follows: " Shun the companionship of fools, impertinents, or meddlers, lest you pass for the same. Never indulge in buffoonery, scandals, deceit, or falsehood. Be frank, generous, and brave; be obliging and kind; study neatness in your dress,

---

* Rutherford (John), *The Troubadours, their Loves and Lyrics*, p. 4. London, 1873.

and let elegance of fashion make up for plainness of
material. Never allow a seam to remain ripped and
gaping; it is worse than a rent; the first shows ill-
breeding, the last only poverty, which is by far the
lesser evil of the two. There is no great merit in
dressing well if you have the means: but a display of
neatness and taste on a small income is a sure token
of superiority of spirit," etc., etc. There is much more
of the same kind, but this citation serves to show how
eminently practical was the advice given to the young
men in olden days.

Very bitter and violent were the attacks made
upon these men by the monks, who were jealous
of the real purity and asceticism of these heretical
Troubadours, and who were infuriated at the publicity
given to their own misdeeds; such an attack is
graphically described by Hueffer in his thoughtful
work on the Troubadours. The writings of "Izarn
the Monk," for instance, he well describes as a "striking specimen of monkish effrontery" and he proceeds
to criticise the "unctuous self-laudation" of his work,
the *Novas del Heretge*, or the *Tale of a Heretic*, a
dialogue between the author and a bishop of the
Albigeois sect.

"The opening lines," says Hueffer, "are important
to the historian of theology. They prove that the
Neo-Manichæan heretics believed, or at least were said
by the Catholics to believe, in something very like
metempsychosis. 'Tell me,' the monk begins, 'in
what school you have learned that the spirit of man,

when it has lost its body, enters an ox, an ass, or a horned wether, a hog, or a hen, whichever it sees first, and migrates from one to the other until a new body of man or woman is born for it? . . . This thou hast taught to deluded people, whom thou hast given to the devil and taken away from God. May every place and every land that has supported thee perish!'"

It is curious and suggestive to find that St. Francis of Assisi had been a Troubadour; Görres† speaks of him as a "genuine Troubadour," and there is no doubt that he and some of his Franciscans were at one time members of the heretical Cathari: indeed it is questionable whether he was at any time an orthodox Churchman, though--like that other Troubadour, Dante—the Church has ever claimed him as a "faithful son."

A few words must now be devoted to what may be termed the general position of the Troubadours, the place and functions of some of them at least. Among the most illustrious of the Troubadours was Alfonso the Second, King of Arragon (1162-1196). Ticknor‡ says: "From 1209 to 1229, the shameful war which gave birth to the Inquisition was carried on with extraordinary cruelty against the Albigenses, a religious sect in Provence, accused of heresy, but persecuted rather by an implacable political ambition.

---

* Hueffer (Francis), *The Troubadours*, p. 32. London, 1878.

† Görres (J.), *Der heilige Franciskus von Assisi, ein Troubadour*. Strassburg, 1826.

‡ Ticknor (George), *History of Spanish Literature*, i., p.p. 284 285. 1849.

To this sect—which in some points opposed the pretensions of the See of Rome, and was at last exterminated by a crusade under the Papal Authority—belonged nearly all the contemporary Troubadours, whose poetry is full of their sufferings and remonstrances.* In their great distress, the principal ally of the Albigenses and Troubadours was Peter the Second of Arragon, who in 1213 perished nobly fighting in their cause at the disastrous battle of Muret. When therefore the Troubadours of Provence were compelled to escape from the burnt and bloody ruins of their homes, not a few of them hastened to the friendly Court of Arragon, sure of finding themselves protected, and their art held in honour, by princes who were at the same time poets." These passages and the accompanying notes are of importance to students, for they show how intimate a part was played by the Troubadours in the religious movements of the period; and how they were instruments in keeping the mystic teaching alive, and in handing on the Wisdom of the east clothed in this, its latest, poetical disguise.

In Germany also the Troubadours dwelt in high places, for, according to M. de Saint-Peloie, the Baron

---

* The following note is given by this author: "Sismondi (*Hist. des Français*, Paris, 8vo. tom. vi. and vii. 1823, 1826), gives an ample account of the cruelties and horrors of the war of the Albigenses, and Llorente (*Histoire de l'Inquisition*, Paris, 1817, tom. i., p. 43), shows the connection of that war with the origin of the Inquisition. The fact that nearly all the Troubadours took part with the persecuted Albigenses is equally notorious. *Histoire Litt. de la France*, tom. xviii., p. 588.

Zurlandben had just (1773) found a MS. in the library of the King, containing the sonnets of princely Troubadours, written about the twelfth and thirteenth centuries. Among these royal writers were the Emperor Henry VI., Conradin, King of Bohemia, and other Princes, Electors, Dukes and Margraves.

The emotional life of the young European nations was largely educated by means of the chivalric romances, based, as they were, on the highest religious and mystic teaching; and later, in 1400-1500, the Celestial Chivalry was the great standard set before the people, as a national ideal.

Says Ticknor :* " Religious romances were written. . . . in the form of Allegories, like the 'Celestial Chivalry,' the 'Christian Chivalry,' 'The Knight of the Bright Star'"; and this author remarks that the object of that interesting book—the *Celestial Chivalry*, written by Hierónimo de San Pedro (at Valencia, in 1554) was to drive out of the world "the profane books of chivalry."

The titles he uses are worth attention, the first part being called " The Root of the Fragrant Rose "; the second, " The Leaves of the Rose." The names are suggestive, for it was just at this period, when, owing to bitter persecution, the Cathari and Albigenses were nearly exterminated,† that the Rosicrucians

---

* Ticknor (George), *Hist. of Spanish Literature*, i. 220, 221. London, 1849.

† "By order of the same François I., his General Almeida extirpated with a cruelty unusual even in those times, the remnant of the Albigenses still lurking in the villages of Provence, a sect, it should be remembered,

THE TROUBADOURS. 133

began to revive the same old Eastern tradition, and the blessed Christian Rosencreutz turned his steps eastwards, and in Arabia spent three years fitting himself for the work to come.

The Rose was one of the ancient traditional mystic symbols, re-adapted by the Rosicrucians, and used, indeed, by all sectaries and mystics Aroux* asserts that the famous *Roman de la Rose*† was not only a satire against the Pontifical Court, but also the apotheosis of heresy, for it contained the Hermetic Science under the guise of a religious poem.

Rossetti ‡ is as emphatic about this symbolic language, and Warton § gives us the following suggestive hints : " In the preface of the edition [to this poem,] printed in the year 1583, all this allegory is turned to religion. The Rose is proved to be a state of grace or divine wisdom, or eternal beatitude, or the Holy Virgin to which heretics cannot gain

---

of genuine Manichæans, transplanted thither from the east at a comparatively recent date. As Manichæans, they would naturally have preserved the symbols and tokens for mutual recognition so much in vogue, as history and existing monuments attest." King M.A. (C. W.), *The Gnostics and their Remains*, p. 399. London, 1887.

* Aroux (Eugène), *Dante, Hérétique, Révolutionnaire et Socialiste*, p. 83. Paris, 1854.

† Begun by Guillaume de Loris—a Troubadour—1260, finished by Jean de Meung, Poet, Alchemist, and Astrologer. It is a Hermetic treatise of much value.

‡ Rossetti (Gabriele), *Il Mistero dell'Amor Platonico del Medio Evo*, ii. 411-414. London, 1840.

§ Warton (Thomas), *Hist. of English Poetry*, II., p. 149, note *d*. London, 1840.

access. It is the White Rose of Jericho, ... the chemists made it a search for the Philosopher's Stone." There is ever a mystery in the crucified Rose, typical of light and glory springing from the blood of Adonis, himself Dionysus, the best of heavenly beings. Endless are the exquisitely beautiful and refined symbolic meanings of the sacred Rose.

Thus as we study the Troubadours it becomes evident that an enormous under-current of secret teaching was being carried on, and Rutherford gives us some important hints on this point which have been previously noticed* but may again be usefully referred to since they illustrate this particular fact and verify much that is said by Aroux.

The body of the learned in the Middle Ages—or the inner circle of that body—seems to have formed a secret society, whose purpose was to keep as much knowledge as possible confined to itself, after the manner of the Druids, or of the Egyptians and Chaldæn Sages; when compelled to put the more occult portions of their scientific acquirements into a more permanent form they adopted one perfectly unintelligible to the vulgar. Some wrapped up their more valuable secrets in parables, others threw them again into the shape of illuminations, and others again adopted the device of Roger Bacon, who, giving the name of an important ingredient of gunpowder in an anagram, rendered the whole receipt for the composition of the substance a complete mystery to the uninitiated.

---

* *The Theosophical Review*, xxiv. 202. London, 1899.

It has been said that Rutherford has allied the Troubadours with the Freemasons, and the latter body has an undoubtedly Manichæan tradition. For confirmation on this point we can refer to what is said by a very well-known Masonic authority,* whose knowledge about Masonry is unquestionable :

Sons of the Widow†—a powerful society founded by Manes, a Persian slave . . . . and continued to the present day; it consisted of two degrees: 1. Auditor. 2. Elect. It was at peace under the Mother of the Emperor Anastasius (A.D. 491-518), but was persecuted by Justin. In the course of time, its agents secretly instigated the Crusades; but being betrayed, had to veil their mysteries under many names. In Bulgaria and Lombardy it was known as the Society of the Paterini, in France as the Cathari and Albigenses, and from it originated the Hussites, Wyckliffites, and Lollards. The Dutch sect of the Family of Love also sprang from it.

Such is the statement of a high Mason on this connection, corroborating the links that have already been outlined, and many more might be instanced, showing that all the tenets of these mediæval sects of Troubadours are traceable to Gnostic and Manichæistic doctrines. Very wonderful is the part filled by the " Messengers of Love " in the spiritual evolution of Europe during the Dark Ages. Martyrs many,

---

* Mackenzie (Kenneth R. H., ix°), *The Royal Masonic Cyclopædia*, p. 768. New York, 1898.

† This term is applied to the Albigensian Troubadours ; and it was employed amongst themselves.

and Saints not a few—such will be the roll-call of the Minniesängers, Troubadours, and Bards of these olden days, when in the future the Ancient Wisdom once more reigns supreme.

THE HEAVENLY KINGDOM OF THE HOLY GRAIL.

PART I.

> AND like a flying star
> Led on the gray-haired Wisdom of the East.
> . . . . .
> I saw the spiritual city and all her spires
> And gateways in a glory like one pearl—
> No larger, tho' the goal of all the Saints—
> Strike from the sea; and from the star there shot
> A rose-red sparkle to the city, and there
> Dwelt, and I knew it was the Holy Grail,
> . . . . .
> Which was an image of the mighty world.
> —*The Holy Grail* and *The Passing of Arthur*,
> TENNYSON.

THE legend of the founding of the City Spiritual—the Kingdom of the Holy Grail* or San Grëal— is so interwoven with myth and superadded tradition that to trace its origin is as difficult as to see through a dense fog the delicate outline of some fair gothic

---

* See *The Theosophical Review*, xxiii., pp. 9-16. Hardcastle (Miss A. L. B.), "The Secret of the Holy Grail."

spire whose lofty head towers beyond the mists towards the blue heights above. But as we gaze with straining effort, slowly through the gloom line upon line reveals itself, and finally the whole structure takes form most definite before us. Thus is it with the priceless "Legend of the Holy Grail," and as we trace it back from Western lands to its Eastern home, gradually from the mists of time's obscurity there stands revealed once more the glorious tradition of the Wisdom Religion, another messenger from East to West bringing the ancient mystic teaching from the old worlds to the new.

In this case the gracious message is vestured, not as usual in religious forms, but veiled in garb of chivalry, so that it may, perhaps, in this new presentation more readily touch the hearts of men, and draw them to seek for the Kingdom Spiritual, the "house not made with hands, eternal in the heavens."

Gathered round the "Holy Grail" are the Knights —the guardians of the "Grail Kingdom," led by Titurel,* the mystic King, to whom is entrusted the charge of the Holy Teaching. Then later we find the Knights Templars taking up the sacred mission.†

---

* Hammer-Purgstall (Baron J. von), *Fundgruben des Orients*, vi. 24., n. 33. Vienna, 1818.

† See Naef (F.), *Opinions religieuses des Templiers*, p. 36. Nismes; 1890. "The cult with which this mysterious chalice is surrounded far surpasses in grandeur and exaltation the worship paid by the Church even to the most sacred relics, and it is just this exaltation of mystery and of holiness which unveils so clearly the symbol and the allegory." And again p. 38, "In the Grail does one not see the

But everywhere and always is there the inner doctrine for the few who seek the Holy Grail, for it is invisible to all but those who form the "Ingesinde"* (inner circle).

The chief function of the Grail Kingdom was to supply a constant type of a divinely governed society, a society ruled from the inner and spiritual planes, and to train in "the kingly art of ruling"

---

striking symbol of Mystic Wisdom *(Sagesse mystique)* and of the communion which is established between God and man?"

* J. Rutherford writes (*The Troubadours, their Loves and Lyrics*, p. 43. London, 1873):

"The body of the learned in the Middle Ages—or the inner circle of that body—seems to have formed a secret society, whose purpose was to keep as much knowledge as possible confined to itself, after the manner of the Druids, or of the Egyptians and Chaldean Sages; when compelled to put the more occult portions of their scientific acquirements into a permanent form, they adopted one perfectly unintelligible to the vulgar. Some wrapped up their more valuable secrets in parables, others threw them again into the shape of illuminations, and others again adopted the device of Roger Bacon, who, giving the name of an important ingredient of gunpowder in an anagram, rendered the whole receipt for the composition of the substance a complete mystery to the uninitiated.

"Our reading shows us that much more was known to the few, six or seven hundred years ago, than modern *savants* are inclined to think. Strange and startling glimpses of this knowledge flicker over the pages of the poets and romancists of the Middle Ages. Selecting but two examples from many, we may remark that no one could have written that passage in the *Inferno* of Dante (Canto xxxiv., lines 70-84), descriptive of the transit of Virgil and his follower through the centre of the earth, who was not well acquainted with the leading principles of the theory of gravitation, as elaborated by Newton. Nor could any one have evolved from the depths of his internal consciousness a passage so singularly anticipative of the discovery of America as that contained in Stanzas 228-230 of the twenty-fifth canto of the *Morgante Maggiore*—precisely the Canto in which it is said that the author, Pulci, was aided by the erudite Marsilio Ficino." See Cantù (Cesare), *Gli Eretici d'Italia*, i. 178. Torino, 1865.

leaders for such communities as needed them. It was destined to be a practical civilizing power as well as a Palace Spiritual, not a passive force only, but active and powerful for the suppression of all evil on earth. Titurel* is the type and ideal leader round whom revolves the whole of mystic or celestial chivalry.† The Grail kingship is indeed the paradigm of the highest perfection, " the goal of all the saints," but the goal cannot be reached except by the conquest of the lower nature; every human being must struggle and must suffer ere he sees

> those shores
> Where tideless sweep the waves of time
> Hard by the city of the saints of God.

Let us now trace the origin of this time-honoured tradition, the stock from which developed all the "Arthurian" legends, all the "Graal-sagas" of Germany, and the "Romans" of Provence. Two dominant variants of the earliest traditions have come to us.

1. The Grail as a Secret Gospel ‡ or Tradition.

---

* There are two Titurels; the poem *Titurel* of Wolfram von Eschenbach; and, later, *Der Jüngere Titurel*, by Albrecht von Scharffenberg, written about 1270. An interesting notice on the subject is given by Vilmar (A. F. C.), *Geschichte der deutschen National-Literatur*, 147, Marburg u. Leipsig, 1870.

† Chivalry was divided into Heavenly and Earthly orders during part of the Middle Ages, especially in Spain.

‡ Aroux (E.), *Les Mystères de la Chevalerie*, p. 166. Paris, 1858. Paris (A. Paulin), *Les Romans de la Table Ronde*, Addenda to p. 102. Vol. I. Paris, 1868. *Helinandi Op.*, Ed. Migne, *Patrol.*, Vol. CCXII., col. 814. Fauriel (C. C.), *Histoire de la Poésie Provençale*, ii. 332, *et seq*. Paris, 1846.

THE HOLY GRAIL.

2. The Grail as a Mystic Cup* with miraculous power.

Both variants are of vital interest to the theosophic student; we must here, however, confine ourselves to tracing.

I. The earliest sources of the Grail Legend.

II. The history of Titurel, the type of divine kingship and spiritual knighthood.

III. The links which prove this popular mystic legend to be part of the great Wisdom tradition which is guarded by the " Masters of Wisdom " yet on this earth.

I.

THE ORIGIN OF THE TRADITION.—I.

This can be definitely followed through Arabia to India; for according to a large number of authorities,† the tradition is mainly Eastern in origin,

---

* Burnouf (Émile) writes as follows : " La vraie légende du Vase Sacré est celle qu'on peut suivre dans le passé en remontant d'aujourd'hui même par les textes chrétiens, grecs, perses et bouddhiques jusqu' aux hymnes du Véda, où elle trouve son explication." *Le Vase Sacré et ce qu'il contient*—dans l'Inde, la Perse, la Gréce, et dans l'Eglise chrétienne avec un appendice sur le Saint-Graal, p. 189. Paris, 1896.

* *The Theosophical Review*, xxiii. pp. 12-15. London, 1899. Hammer-Purgstall (Baron J. von), *Fundgruben des Orients*, vi. p. 24. Rio, *L'Université Catholique*, i. p. 241.

† Rosenkranz (Dr. Karl), *Handbuch einer Allgemeinen Geschichte der Poesie*, ii., 84. Halle, 1832. Hagen (F. H. von der), *Heldenbilde aus dem Sagen Kreisen*, II., iii. 8. Breslau, 1823. Simrock (Dr. K.), *Parzifal und Titurel*, p. 484. Stuttgart und Tübingen, 1842. Bergmann (Dr. F. G.), *The San Grëal; an Enquiry into the Origin and Signification of the San Grëal*. Edinburgh, 1870. Bartsch (Karl), *Wolfram von Eschenbach—Parzifal und Titurel*, pt. i. p. xxiv. Leipzig, 1870. Vilmar (A. F. C.), *Geschichte der Deutschen National-Literatur*, i. 129-130. Marburg and Leipzig, 1870.

especially that of the Gral-king and Founder, with which are linked most intimately those of Parsifal and Lohengrin. Rosenkranz divides them as follows: Titurel is Oriental in its inception; Parsifal is Gallic (from Anjou); and Lohengrin* is Belgian.

The most sympathetic and interesting version perhaps, is that given by Görres† in his introduction to the translation of the oldest MS. which is in the Vatican Library. This manuscript was seen by von Hagen,‡ who gives an interesting account of it in his letters; another sketch of the Gral-saga, but less sympathetic, is given by Dr. Bergman in a small pamphlet printed in 1870. From all these various sources must be gathered the important fragments which will help us to find those details which are a necessity to the student for a clear understanding of the real meaning of this grand old legend.

Our attention must first be directed to what may be termed the "setting" of the tradition, that is to say the channel by which it comes to the Western world. The record of Titurel was first made known by Wolfram von Eschenbach, a Troubadour of a noble but poor family; born within the

---

* The history of Lohengrin, or Garin-le-Loherain was first treated by Hugo Metullus, in 1150.

† Görres (Joseph), *Lohengrin, ein altdeutsches Gedicht nach der Abschrift des Vaticanischen Manuscriptes, von Ferdinand Glöckle herausgegeben.* 1813.

Koberstein (A.), *Grundriss zur Geschichte der Deutschen National-Literatur*, p. 50. Leipzig, 1830.

‡ Hagen (F. H. von der), *Briefe in die Heimat*, ii. 305. Breslau, 1818.

THE HOLY GRAIL.

last thirty years of the twelfth century, he died about 1220; his monument was still existing at Eschenbach in Bavaria in the fifteenth century. He was one of a brilliant circle of Troubadours or Minnesänger* who at that period were gathered at the then famous Court of Herman, Landgraf of Thuringia. Wolfram began a history in verse of Titurel, the old Gral-king, which was however left in an unfinished and fragmentary condition at his death. Then about the year 1270, Albrecht von Schaffenberg wrote a poem upon Titurel which for long passed as the work of von Eschenbach. It was called *Der Jüngere Titurel*, to distinguish it from the original poem of Wolfram. Speaking of it San Marte† says:

Titurel—two fragments to which, according to the opening lines of the first piece, this title has been given, should according to Wolfram von Eschenbach's own assurances have formed part of a history of Sigune and Schiantulander, for it stands in close relation to Parzifal, the material having been drawn from the same source—remained unfinished. That work, however, and especially the sayings of the Holy Grail contained therein, aroused such excitement, that after Wolfram's death an unknown poet decided to write, in strophe form, the history of the Gral and its race of kings (Titurel), in accordance with the same source. . . . This also remained unfinished until

---

* *Trouvères* in Northern France; *Troubadours* in the South of France; *Minnesänger* in Germany; *Skalds* or *Scalds* in Norway; *Bards* in Wales and Ancient Britain.

† San Marte (A. Schulz), *Leben und Dichten von W. v. Eschenbach*, xiv. Magdeburg, 1836.

about 1270, when a certain Albrecht completed it. This so-called *Jüngere Titurel* and the *Parzifal*, both of which come from the same source, contain pretty well the whole history of the Holy Grail and in many passages they supplement one another. *

These form undoubtedly the most authentic versions of the Gral legend, but there is another line of tradition written down by Chrestien de Troyes, which eliminates the oriental and gives the purely Christian version of the vision of Joseph of Arimathæa. Of this Wolfram was cognizant, or, as Nutt† tells us,

He knew Chrestien's poem well, and repeatedly refers to it, but with great contempt, as being the wrong version of the story, whereas he holds the true version from Kyot‡ the singer, a "Provenzal," who found the tale of Parzifal

---

* The fragments of "Titurel" written by Wolfram were first made known by Docens (1810). They are in Karl Lachmann's edition of Wolfram v. Eschenbach (1833). The only edition of the *Jüngere Titurel*, which exists in a good many MSS., is that of Hahn (1842).

† Nutt (Alfred), *Studies on the Legend of the Holy Grail*, p. 6. London, 1888. See *The Theosophical Review*, xxiii. 10.

‡ Many materialistic critics have tried to disprove the very existence of Kyot (or Guiot de Provins), and further have tried to prove that the tradition was invented by Wolfram. But research shows definitely that at this very period there was a *Jongleur*, or singer, of this name. He is mentioned by the Abbé de la Rue in his *Essais historiques sur les Bardes, les Jongleurs, et les Trouvères*, i. 216. Caen, 1834. In this passage is mentioned a Satire written by Guiot de Provins; Rosenkranz also mentions him in his *Handbuch einer Allgemeinen Geschichte der Poesie*, ii. 114. The same conclusion has also been arrived at by San Marte in an interesting article "Der Mythus vom Heiligen Gral," which appeared in the *Neue Mittheilungen aus dem Gebiet historisch antiquarischer Forschungen*. Herausgegeben von dem Thuringisch-Sæchsichen

written in a heathen tongue at Dolêt (Toledo) by Flegetanis, a heathen, and who first wrote concerning the Grail, put it into French, and after searching the chronicles of Britain, France, and Ireland in vain, at length found the information in the chronicle of Anjou.

Later on we shall see why it was found in these chronicles to the exclusion of the rest. The basis of the Christian legend is from the Gnostic tradition, and said to have been founded on the Apocryphal Gospel of Nicodemus, which was translated into Provençal verse, a "mystical Gospel" in every sense, says Paulin Paris,* who, in referring to the MS. in the Vatican, further writes : " This latter text was of great antiquity and evidently mystical, showing a profound knowledge of the Apocryphal† Gospels containing the secret teachings of the Eucharist."‡ This of course refers to the Christian aspect, and had to do with the Christian arcane doctrines, but this aspect must be left for treatment at some future time.

A digression, however, must be here made, the subject of which is so intimately interwoven with the

---

Verein für Erforschung des Vaterländischen Alterthums. (III., pt. iii., pp. 1-40). The author identifies the supposed mythical Guiot von Provence with the historical character Guiot von Provins (the town in Brie ?) which is called *Provîs* by Wolfram.

* Paris (A. Paulin), *Les Manuscrits françois de la Bibliothèque du Roi.* Paris, 1848. Vol. vii., p. 377.

† " Books withdrawn from public perusal, or in other words, hidden or secret." See Mead (G. R. S), " The Secret Sermon on the Mountain," *The Theosophical Review*, xxiv. 26.

‡ See Fauriel (C. C.), *Histoire de la Poésie Provençale*, iii. 5. Paris, 1846.

mystic foundation of the Grail that it is necessary to go into some important details in order to form a clear conception of the many forces which were at play during this epoch.

It has been said that Wolfram von Eschenbach,* the writer of *Titurel*, was a Troubadour, and according to some authorities Guiot (or Kyot) de Provins was a Jongleur. Who, then, are these Troubadours and Jongleurs who played a part so important in the so-called dark ages? On another occasion we hope to take up this subject separately, forming as it does an important link between eastern mysticism and western development; it will be enough for the present to cite one important Catholic writer, who makes a very clear statement as to the hidden functions of these Troubadours.† Says Aroux:

The Troubadours, hostile to Rome, were, to say the

---

* Mysticism was "in the air" at this epoch; in Calabria the Abbate Gioachimo di Flor was preaching his *Evangelio Eterno*. Educated at the Court of the Duca di Puglia, a pilgrim to the Holy Land, a monk at Mount Tabor, he became a mystic and was according to Cantù deeply tinged with Buddhistic views (*Gli Eretici d'Italia*, i. 120-135. Torino, 1865). He had a large following. A quantity of important writings were left by this great mystic. His prophecies were known even in England, for we find an English Cistercian, Rudolph, Abbot of Coggeshall, coming to Rome in 1195, had a conference with him, and left an account of it (Martène, *Amplissima Collectio*, v. 837), and Felice Tocco (*L'Eresia nel Medio Evo*, i. 261-409. Florence, 1884) writes: "The works of Joachim were printed at Venice in the years 1517-19, and his life was written by a Dominican named Gervaise in 1745. A full summary of his opinions, and those contained in *The Everlasting Gospel*, may be found in Natalis Alexander's *Ecclesiastical History*, VIII., pp. 73-76."

† Aroux (Eugène) *Dante, Hérétique, Révolutionnaire et Socialiste; Révélation d'un Catholique sur le Moyen Age*, p. 14. Paris, 1854.

THE HOLY GRAIL. 147

truth, the journalists of the period; and in this way constituted one of the powers of society and took up sides for republican liberty in the towns of the south, for the feudal suzerainty and its patrons—that is to say chivalry—against the church or authority. . . . for chivalry itself had become a machinery of war on the side of the Albigensian* heresy.

Strange and striking statements, but they can be tested and verified by testimony from all sides. Through these secret mystical channels came pouring the old teachings from the East, and Wolfram von Eschenbach and Guiot de Provins were but instruments or channels for that tradition.

A few words must here be said about Guiot, or, as Wolfram von Eschenbach calls him in his German tongue, Kyot. As we have seen from the Abbé de la Rue, he was a Jongleur, and Aroux has given a clue as to the real *métier* of the true Jongleur at that period. He appears to have been a native of the Duchy of Anjou, and was not a noble but a lay commoner, for Wolfram terms him simply *Meister*. Guiot studied literature and philosophy in the south of France in the Province of Saint Giles—a centre of Albigensian mystic tradition, and in constant communication with northern Spain, which was permeated, at this period, with Arabian mysticism. He also studied for some time in Spain at Toledo

---

* The mystic doctrines of the Albigenses will be treated later. They believed in re-incarnation and other fundamental theosophic doctrines.

under the learned Arabian philosophers, to whom the Western world owes a heavy debt. Meister Guiot le Provençal found at Toledo an Arabian book compiled by an astrologer and philosopher named Flegetanis,* containing the story of the Holy Grëal. This volume was written in a foreign character, of which Guiot was compelled to make himself master. After reading this Guiot began to search the records of other countries, Brittany, France, Ireland, and he found the legends of this in some old *Chroniques d' Angevin* (Anjou). These he used as corroboration, and introduces the Western elements into his history, but, as Warton and Görres both insist, the scene for the most part is laid in the East, and a large proportion of the names are of oriental origin. Then, again, the Saracens are always spoken of with consideration; Christian knights enroll themselves under the banner of the Caliph,† and no trace of hatred is to be found between the followers of the crescent and the cross. Speaking of the widespread development of this mysterious legend, or tradition of the Holy Grail, Görres ‡ says:

From the waters of the Ganeas (Ganges) in the land

---

* Flegetanis was both an astronomer and an astrologer. Both Görres and Warton (Thomas Warton, *The History of English Poetry*, Vol. I., London, 1824) consider that Flegetanis is a corruption of the Arabic name Felek-daneh, an astronomer.

† It can be proved from various sources that there was a friendly interchange of visits between the Caliph at Cairo and the Templars. (King, C. W., *The Gnostics and their Remains*, p. 418. London, 1887.)

‡ *Lohengrin*, p. ix.

of Tribalibot, that is Palibothra* in Tricalinga, the Sanskrit name of the Ganges Provinces, it has spread itself over the Caucasus, or as the poem more correctly says, Kukkhasus, or again, as Titurel says, Kaukasus, where the red gold grows, from which the heathen weave many a beautiful coat (Wat) and over the mountains Agrimontin, where the warm Salamanders weave their glittering uniform amid the fire-flames' dance, and where the Queen Gekurdille rules.

Everywhere can be found the tradition of a sacred cup,† and it is said by Flegetanis, who had carefully recorded the result of his nocturnal studies at Toledo, that this mysterious cup‡ with the name of Graal emblazoned on it was left behind on earth by a band of spirits§ as they winged their way to their celestial abode. This holy vessel is delivered by an angel to Titurel, at whose birth an angel had announced that God had chosen him to be a defender of the faith ||

---

* "Pâtaliputra (Palibothra des Grecs) qui est aujourd'hui Patna." Burnouf, *op. cit.* p. 109.

† In the Persian tradition a similar miraculous and mystical vessel was given to Jemshad, the pattern of perfect kings, in whose reign the Golden Age was realised in Iran. He was the favourite of Ormuzd and his legitimate representative on earth; he discovered the "Goblet of the Sun" when digging the foundation of Persepolis, and from him it passed to Alexander the Great. It is a symbol of the world. See Burnouf (Émile), *Le Vase Sacré et ce qu'il contient. Dans l'Inde, la Perse, la Grèce et dans l'Eglise chrétienne*, p. 189. Paris, 1896.

‡ In Grecian mythology Apollo, or Helios, rises out of a golden-winged cup.

§ Blavatsky (H. P.) *The Secret Doctrine*, ii. 379: "The beneficent Entities who . . . brought light to the world, and endowed Humanity with intellect and reason."

|| The Gnosis, or Wisdom Mysteries.

and the guardian of the Sangrëal. He became, in fact, one of the custodians of that Secret Wisdom which has been left in the charge of the elect, the group of humanity's perfected sons.

THE HEAVENLY KINGDOM OF THE HOLY GRAIL.

PART II.

THE ORIGIN OF THE TRADITION.—II.

> . . . THE Grail, throughout all Ages, may never by man be known,
> Save by him God calleth to It, whose name God doth know alone.
> And the tale shall be told in all lands . . . .
> *Parzival*, translated by J. L. WESTON, i. 162.

> WE must trace the history of the World-Religion, alike through the secret Christian sects as through those of other great religious subdivisions of the race; for the Secret Doctrine is the Truth, and that religion is nearest divine that has contained it with the least adulteration. Our search takes us hither and thither, but never aimlessly do we bring sects, widely separated in chronological order, into critical juxtaposition. There is one purpose in our work to be kept constantly in view—the analysis of religious beliefs, and the definition of their descent from the past to the present.
> BLAVATSKY (H. P.), *Isis Unveiled*, ii., 292.

IT is now necessary to add some more important details to the question of the origin of the tradition of the Holy Grail. Too much care cannot be given by students to the most fundamental portion of this research.

It has already been said that many German* and French writers, in their zealous efforts to prove the Grail tradition to be a myth, have made efforts to disprove the existence of Guiot von Provins, but owing to the careful researches of San Marte† there is evidence of his existence so conclusive that no further doubt can remain; in the review from which we quote he gives a careful *résumé* of the evidence, and he has made a thorough study of Guiot's *Bible*, which was written as a denunciation of the priests of that period, and of the iniquities of the Roman Church: "Guiot was, without doubt, a learned man, and had been a monk as well as a courtier," says San Marte, from whose article the following summary is made.

He was present in the year 1184, at Mainz, at the great court day of the Emperor Frederick I., at which the French nobility were also present in great numbers. He further assures us that he had seen the Hospitallers at Jerusalem; the information he gives us as regards the Knight Templars in Syria will consequently rest likewise on first-hand observation. In the east‡ he saw King Amalrich of

---

* Lachmann (K.), *Wolfram von Eschenbach*, xxiv., and Gervinus, *Deutsche National Literatur*, i., 358, 1835, are both of this opinion.

† San Marte (A. Schulz), "Wolfram von Eschenbach and Guiot von Provins"; *Germania*, iii. 445. Wien, 1860.

‡ This fact that Guiot von Provins was himself in the East, that he was, moreover, a Troubadour, gives us those links which were needed to prove the direct connection of this Grail Tradition with the Eastern Wisdom; as a Troubadour he was one of the Secret Society already

THE HOLY GRAIL.

Jerusalem, who died in the year 1173, in the flower of his age and his glory. But in the year 1147 there was the second, and in the year 1190 the third Crusade . . . . it may be inferred from his writing that he journeyed into the Holy Land, not as a warrior, but in the retinue of a Prince or Baron, and we learn that Guiot was also in the monastery of Clairvaux,* and moreover, when he wrote his *Bible* he had already worn the black cowl for more than twelve years; thus his denunciations would rest on personal observations, and not on any mere gossip or scandal.

Guiot shows himself, in this writing, to be a man of scholarly education, of penetrating mind, keen observation and full of biting sarcasm. His comparisons and examples are of incisive acuteness, he has an exact knowledge of the Bible, and brings forward passages from the Scriptures in confirmation of his judgment, and in justification of his reproaches of the clergy. To quote again from San Marte:

His language is incisive and severe . . . . . pouring out his noble anger, galling blame and bitter sarcasm, over priests and nobles, higher and lower clergy,

---

mentioned both by Rossetti in his *Disquisitions on the Anti-papal Spirit which produced the Reformation*, (ii., 115. London, 1834), and by Aroux; see *The Theosophical Review*, xxiv., p. 207. San Marte added a footnote stating that he was preparing an edition of Guiot's *Bible* and Lyric Poems, in French and German, to which Professor G. Wohlfart was adding notes.

* S. Bernard of Clairvaux was one of the Church Mystics of the twelfth century; he gave the first rules to the Order of the Knights-Templars, the regulations having been arranged at the Council of Troyes in 1118. The great Abbey of Clairvaux was one of the chief centres of education at this period. S. Bernard considered the contemplative life as the highest, and he was himself a contemplative mystic.

and over pretended erudition, he nevertheless loves to add that, of course, there are glorious exceptions. . . . We perceive in him a mind which, formed in the school of life, has seen and experienced much; a man who with keen vision and solid judgment watched and weighed the crimes of all positions. . . . He very clearly distinguishes genuine piety from the hypocritical appearance of holiness—the true faith from professional sanctity. . . . Truth is for him beyond all else; it is his light.

Such is the judgment of this well-known German author upon the man through whom the tradition comes. Miss Weston, another authority, says:

Such a man would have been thoroughly familiar with the legends that had gathered round the early Angevin Princes, as well as with the historical facts connected with their successors; he would have come into contact with the Order of the Knights Templars . . . he would be familiar with many a legend of precious stones, the favourite talismans of the East, and would know the special virtue ascribed to each. . . . In fact, if we will allow the existence of such a writer as a travelled Angevin might well have been, we shall find all the principal problems of the Parzifal admit of a rational explanation. Even the central puzzle, Wolfram's representation of the Grail, is explicable on such a hypothesis. We know how very vague Chrêtien's* account of the Grail is; how much in the dark he leaves us as to Its outward form, Its influence and its origin. A writer before Chrêtien is scarcely likely to have been more explicit; what more likely than that a man long resident in the east, and familiar, as has been said above, with eastern jewel talismans, and the legends connected with them, when

---

* Troyes (Chrêtien de), *Li conte del Graal.* 1189.

confronted with this mysterious Grail, of which no definite account was given, yet which apparently exercised a magical life-sustaining influence, should have jumped to the conclusion of Its, at least partial, identity with the precious stones of the power of which he had heard so much?

Then later on the same writer says:

To sum up the entire question, the drift of the internal evidence of the Parzival seems to indicate that the author of Wolfram's Source was a warm partisan of the House of Anjou,* sometime resident in the East, familiar with the history of the House whose fortunes he followed, and with much curious oriental lore, and thoroughly imbued with the broader views of life and religion inspired by the crusades. That he wrote his poem after 1172 seems most likely from the connection between England, Anjou and Ireland noted in Book IX; . . . if we grant the correctness of the Angevin allusions to be found in the earlier parts of the poem, we must logically grant that these two first books, and as a consequence the latter part of the poem which agrees with them, are due to the French source rather than the German redaction; that it was Kiot (Guiot de Provins) who introduced the characters of Gamuret, Belakané, Feirefis and Lâhelein; that to Kiot is due the first germ of the ethical interpretation amplified by Wolfram. It was probably in a great measure owing to the unecclesiastical nature of Kiot's teaching, and the freedom with which he handled the Grail myth, that his work failed to attain the popularity of Chrêtien's. When the Grail legend was once definitely stamped with the traditional

---

* He was in the retinue of Fulk of Anjou, who, in 1129, became the son-in-law of Baldwin, King of Jerusalem, and eventually became its King. There is, however, a much earlier connection of the House of Anjou with the East, for in 987 Fulk Nerra, or Fulk the Palmer, went to Jerusalem. See *Croniques des Comtes d'Anjou*, par M. Émile Mabille, p. lxxviii. Paris, 1856.

Christian character which it finally assumed and retained, the semi-pagan character of Kiot's treatment would cause his version to be regarded with disfavour by the monkish compilers of his day.*

There is no difficulty in perceiving that the Christian version has become the more popular, almost to the extinction of the oriental tradition, but the suggestion here made by the writer is of importance—for Guiot, having been in contact with the Secret and Mystical Societies in the East, would certainly bring that doctrine into his work, which accounts for what Miss Weston terms the "uneccle-siastical nature of Kiot's (Guiot) teaching."

It is an important fact for the students of this tradition to bear in mind, that the Roman Church monopolized and adopted this Legend of the Holy Grail, laying stress upon the version given by Chrêtien de Troyes, ignoring its oriental descent, and popularizing the idea that the Legend was founded on a purely Christian basis; hence many of the contemporaries of Wolfram von Eschenbach were writing solely from the Christian standpoint; but we have also many writers who took a broader view, and who recognized that the tradition had descended from some earlier doctrine. In San Marte (A. Schulz), for instance, we have a German scholar of profound research adopting practically the same view as that of Eugene Aroux in his *Mystères de la Chevalerie*, to which book reference was made in the

---

* Weston (Jessie L.), *Parzival*, ii. 191, 197, 198. London, 1894.

last number. We must now summarize some important passages from this new source, relating as they do to the same view, namely, that the Legend of the Holy Grail is, in truth, part of the mystical tradition of those so-called heretical sects, the Albingenses, the Cathari, and others of that date, descendants of the older Gnostic Sects. Says San Marte:

The conflicts of the Hohenstaufen with Rome bear witness to the strength of this movement in Germany; princes, knights and poets accepted* it with fullest consciousness [of its significance]. Guiot's *Bible*, and other similar writings, the Provençal poets, the numerous heretical sects of Southern France, of Northern Italy and Spain prove the same thing regarding these countries. Among the Waldensians there even gradually arose, under the influence of the Provençal poets, a literature, the content of which was chiefly spiritual, and which, in a poetical form, made the peculiar principles of the sect current and familiar among the people.† We may mention the

---

* The writer is referring to the enormous spread of these mystical and heretical teachers. See San Marte (A. Schulz), "Wolfram's Parzival und seine Beurtheiler," in *Germania*, vii., p. 60. Wien, 1862.

† This was the secret language to which Aroux refers so often. In one passage he says: "Let the philologists make as much outcry as they will, our old *Troveurs* knew more about it than they do, and when they adopted certain names they thought far more of the hidden meaning than of the actual etymology, for which they cared very little"; again, referring to the well-known legend of Amadis, "the Knight of the Lion," he adds: "We may easily recognize him, by these various signs, as a 'Poor-man of Lyons.' Like his colleagues, this Apostle of the Albigensian Gospel leaves Aquitanian Gaul, his own country, to go into Spain and win over that country to the Religion of Love, as in other romances. What gives an account of his acts and deeds is the journal, the record of his apostolic feats, of his triumph over the agents of Rome. What could be easier to recognise? Amadis, the 'Perfect Knight of Lyons,' under

celebrated didactic poem, written about 1180, *La nobla Leyczon*, which leads up to Waldensian through sacred history, and other poems such as *La Barca, Lo novel Sermon, Lo novel Confort, Lo Payre Eternal, Lo Desprecza del Mont (Contentio Mundi)* and *L'Avangeli de li quatre Semenez*, which deals with the parable, Matthew xiii. 5, of the different seeds. They all possess peculiarly strong anti-papistic elements and belong to those products of anti-hierarchy, which transplanted the conflict against Rome from ecclesiastical domain to the ground of popular life. How wrathful is Bernard of Clairvaux against Abelard ;* he says that, thanks to him, the street-boys of Paris are to be heard discussing the doctrine of the Trinity! It was a storm which raged through the whole of western Christendom in all strata of the population, a process of fermentation which, originally repressed by force, repeated itself in the Reformation and forced itself to the forefront. When, therefore, Reichel † reproaches me with having introduced far more theological elements than the poem itself justifies, into my interpretation of the oracle of the Grail and of Parzival's refraining from questions, I reply that, on the contrary, not nearly enough of the theology of the twelfth century has been applied to the understanding of our poem,

---

disguise of person and language is enamoured of the beautiful Oriane. This name, derived from the East, also indicates the close connection established between the local Vaudism and the oriental Albigensianism typified by the beautiful lady, Flower, Rose, Star of the East. All light, all good, was in this literature reputed to come from the East." Aroux (E.), *Les Mystères de la Chevalerie*, pp. 175, 176. Paris, 1858.

* One of the Scholastic mystics, a heretic, and condemned by the Pope about 1140; he opposed the view of those who extol the faith that yields an unreasoning assent, without examination, to whatever is heard. See Blunt, D.D. (J. H.), article, "Schoolmen"; *Dictionary of Sects and Heresies*, p. 530. London, 1874.

† Reichel, *Studien zu Wolfram's Parzival*, p. 6. Wien, 1858. San Marte (A. Schulz), *Parzival Studien*, Heft ii. Halle; Waisenhaus, 1861.

and my attempt to examine it from that standpoint is only a first beginning on those lines.

For that which we now after the lapse of centuries can only laboriously and yet imperfectly discover about the explanation of the external historical phenomena of those religious conflicts—all that surround the then existing world like a fiery atmosphere in which it breathed, and which penetrated all the pores of its life, the elements of religious discord which can now hardly be understood and methodically arranged by the scholars who make the subject their special study—was formerly in the minds and mouths of the masses and urged them on to action; and if the poems* of that period afford us in almost every other respect a faithful mirror of contemporary phenomena in action and thought, the same must be true of a work which has a predominatingly religious tendency, that finds expression even in the first two lines [of the poem].

It is very desirable that the Church historians of to-day should, in their writings and academic lectures, pay greater attention than they do to the investigations and the treasures which have been brought to light in the ever-increasing study of the early German and French literatures, indeed they would then find much which preceded and led up to the Reformation, and would recognize more clearly the forms taken by the dogmatic theses in the practical faith and opinions of the people, and the special expression which they there received. For there is a difference between the doctrinal formulation of an article of faith and its acceptance and transmission by the laity.

The position taken up by Wolfram, whether Guelph or Ghibelline, Apostolic-Evangelical or Roman-Hierarchic,

---

* The poems of the Troubadours, which contained the mystical teaching, as we have seen from Aroux, in his *Mystères de la Chevalerie*, and also from Rutherford in his *Troubadours, their Loves and Lyrics*, p. 43. London, 1873. See for quotation, *The Theosophical Review*, xxiv., p. 202.

must determine the standpoint from which his poem must be judged and understood. And even if we condemn the poet as a heretic, we must not demand of his poem that it should teach what he rejects,* but in order to do it justice we must enter into his religious tendency, which it brings quite clearly and candidly to light. In view of the historical situation and the religious stream of tendency at the end of the twelfth century the intention of our poet can no longer be open to doubt. He wished, namely, to depict in the institution of the Templars a Christian brotherhood,† a kingdom of the faithful and the elect of the Lord, without a Roman hierarchy, without a Pope and a privileged priesthood, without ban, interdict or Inquisition, where God Himself, through the revelation of the Grail, is, in the spirit of the pure Gospel, Ruler and Judge of His people. He considered the real priesthood to belong to the individuals struggling towards a true knowledge of God, not to an exclusive class, however highly he may have esteemed the latter; finally, he borrowed from the order of the Templars, at that time still flourishing and immaculate, the poetical symbol of the ideal constitution of this brotherhood.

This idea, plainly heretical from the Roman point of view, necessarily implied that the Kingdom of the Grail, which alone led to salvation, stood in quite as sharp a contrast to Roman orthodox Christianity, as represented by the existing visible Church, as it did to paganism;‡ but it is a fine trait in the poet that he is neither led away into open

---

* This is precisely what the dogmatic Christian writers have tried to do by eliminating the Gnostic traces, and the yet more eastern sources of the grand old tradition.

† This is the true Christian Brotherhood open to every soul, the Elect of Humanity, that "Communion of Saints" of which the Great White Lodge is the sole earthly representative.

‡ Even San Marte, in spite of his frankly acknowledged change of position, is still bound by the obsolete views about paganism.

THE HOLY GRAIL. 161

polemic against the ruling Church nor into fanatical hostility to Paganism. There is, therefore, small ground for astonishment at the facts 'that no trace is to be found in the poem of any subordination of the Templars to clergy or Pope,' that Parzival attains to the kingdom of the Grail without any ecclesiastical mediation, and that he did not gain the crown of martyrdom in the conflict, as the fundamental thought of the poet logically demanded.*

This fundamental thought, however, is not based on the Dictatus Gregorii VII. nor on the saying of Innocent III., '*Papa veri Dei vicem gerit in terra*,' but directly on the Gospel and on the saying of the Apostle : ' But ye are a chosen generation—a royal priesthood—a holy nation—a peculiar people ; that ye should show forth the praises of him who hath called you out of darkness into his marvellous light ';† which saying is repeated almost literally in strophes 44 and 45 of Wolfram's *Titurel-fragments*. It is, therefore, inadmissible to regard the Grail as 'a Christian relic,' to make it the representment of the pre-cosmic genesis of Evil, and to speak of 'the spiritual side of the poem' as 'weighed down by the fetishism of the impersonal relic'; this view could only arise through the introduction of evidence regarding Lucifer's fall and the Holy Grail much later than Wolfram's poem, or which—in the cases when this [evidence] is earlier, he does not himself introduce, and which, therefore, must be treated as non-existent in the criticism of our poem. Wolfram makes no special allusion to the dish of Cæsarea‡ used in the Lord's Supper, never speaks of Joseph of Arimathea, nor does he mention the

---

* See *Studies*, l.c., pp. 20 *et seq.*

† 1 Peter, ii., 9, 10.

‡ The "dish of Cæsarea" belongs to the other version, *Joseph of Arimathea*, by Sires Robiers de Borron, which was "englisht" in 1450, by Henry Lonelich. See *The Grand St. Graal*, from Furnivall's edition. Early English Text Society. Trubner, 1874.

Stone of the Grail having been originally in the crown of Lucifer; on the contrary, according to him, it is the *lapis exilis*,* the Stone† of the Lord, which at the beginning of all things was with God.

The symbolism of man as a stone, is the idea that is being expressed by the writer; an ancient idea, and one that is found in almost every religion.

There is one beautiful tradition connected with this legend of the Grail, supposed to have had its origin in Great Britain, and therefore of peculiar interest to us. It is said to have been inscribed in the *Chronicles of Helinandus*, who was "well-known at the time the Romance was written, not only as a historian but as a Troubadour, at one time in high favour at the Court of Philip Augustus, and in later years as one of the most ardent preachers of the Albigensian Crusade."‡ He lived about 1229. The passages here summarized are from Paulin Paris's charming work; the marvellous vision was revealed to a hermit in Britain about 720, and runs thus:

On Holy Thursday of the year 717, after concluding

---

* Writers vary in their spelling of the stone; *Lapis, Lapsit* or *Jaspes, exilles, exilexor, exillis*, and other variants are given. *Lapis Electrix* is given by William Hertz in his *Parzival*, pp. 160, 528. Stuttgart, 1898. He draws attention to the fiery and life-giving properties of the stone. This to some students of Theosophy will be a valuable suggestion.

† In the old symbolism, "Man," chiefly the Inner Spiritual Man, is called a "stone." Christ is called a corner stone, and Peter refers to all men as "lively" (living) stones. Blavatsky (H. P.), *The Secret Doctrine*, ii. 663, 3rd edition. London, 1893.

‡ Evans (Sebastian), *The High History of the Holy Grail*, II., p. 293. London, 1898.

the office of the Tenebrae, I fell asleep, and presently methought I heard in a piercing voice these words:—
"*Awake! Hearken to three in one, and to one in three!*"
I opened my eyes—I found myself surrounded by an extraordinary brightness. Before me stood a man of most marvellous beauty: "Hast thou rightly understood my words?" he said. "Sire, I should not dare to say so." "It is the proclamation of the Trinity. Thou didst doubt whether in the three Persons there were only one God, one only Power. Canst thou now say who I am?" "Sire, my eyes are mortal; Thy great brightness dazzles me, and the tongue of man cannot give utterance to that which is above humanity."

The Unknown bent towards me and breathed upon my face. Thereupon my senses expanded, my mouth was filled with infinity of speech. But when I would fain have spoken I thought I saw bursting forth from my lips a fiery brand which checked the first words I would have uttered.

"Take courage," said the Unknown to me; "I am the source of all truth, the fount of all wisdom. I am the Great Master, he of whom Nicodemus said: 'We know that thou art God.' I come, after confirming thy faith, to reveal to thee the greatest secret in the world."

He then held out to me a book which could easily have been held in the hollow of the hand; "I entrust to you," he said, "the greatest marvel that man can ever receive. This is a book written by my own hand, which must be read with the heart, no mortal tongue being able to pronounce the words without affecting the four elements, troubling the heavens, disturbing the air, rending the earth, and changing the colour of the waters. For every man who shall open it with a pure heart, it is the joy of both body and soul, and whosoever shall see it need have no fear of sudden death, whatever be the enormity of his sins."

The great light that I had already found so hard to

endure then increased until I was blinded by it. I fell, unconscious, and when I felt my senses returning, I no longer saw anything around me, and I should have taken what I had just experienced for a dream, had I not still found in my hand the book that the Great Master had given me. I then arose, filled with sweet joy; I said my prayers, then I looked at the book, and found as its first title: *This is the beginning of thy lineage.* After reading until Prime,* it seemed to me that I had only just begun, so many letters were there in these small pages. I read on again until Tierce, and continued to follow the steps of my lineage, and the record of the good life of my predecessors.

Beside them, I was but the shadow of a man, so far was I from equalling them in virtue. Continuing the book, I read: *Here beginneth the Holy Grail.* Then, the third heading: *This is the beginning of Fears.* Then, a fourth heading: *This is the beginning of Wonders.* A flash of lightning blazed before my eyes, followed by a clap of thunder. The light continued, I could bear its dazzling brightness no longer, and a second time I fell unconscious.

How long I remained thus I do not know. When I arose, I found myself in profound darkness. Little by little, daylight returned, the sun resumed its brightness, I felt myself pervaded by the most delicious scents, I heard the sweetest songs that I had ever listened to; the voices from which they proceeded seemed to touch me, but I neither saw them nor could I reach them. They praised Our Lord, and repeated: *Honour and glory to the Vanquisher of death, to the source of life eternal.*

Having repeated these words eight times, the voices ceased; I heard a great rustling of wings, succeeded by perfect silence; nothing remained but the perfumes whose sweetness entered into me.

---

* Six o'clock in the morning. Tierce corresponds to 9; Sexte, Nones, and Vespers to noon, 3 o'clock and 6 o'clock.

The hour of Nones came, and I thought myself yet at the earliest dawn. Then I closed the book and commenced the service for Good Friday. We do not consecrate on this day, because our Lord chose it for His death. In presence of the reality one should not have recourse to symbol; and if we consecrate on other days, it is in commemoration of the real Sacrifice of the Friday.*

As I was preparing to receive my Saviour, and had already divided the bread into three portions, an angel came, took hold of my hands and said to me: "Thou must not make use of these portions until thou hast beheld what I am about to show thee." Then he raised me into the air, not in the body but in the spirit, and transported me to a place where I was immersed in a joy such as no tongue could tell, no ear could hear, no heart could feel. I should speak no untruth in saying that I was in the third heaven, whither St. Paul was caught up; but that I be not accused of vanity I will merely say that there was revealed to me the great secret which, according to St. Paul, no human speech could utter. The angel said to me: "Thou hast seen great wonders, prepare thyself to see still greater." He carried me higher yet, into a place a hundred times clearer than glass, and a hundred times more brilliant in colouring. There I had a vision of the Trinity, of the distinction between the Father, the Son and the Holy Spirit, and of their union in one and the same form, one and the same Deity, one and the same power. Let not the envious here reproach me with going against the authority of St. John the Evangelist, in that he has told us that *mortal eyes never will or can behold the Eternal Father*, for St. John meant the bodily eyes, whereas the soul can see, when it is

---

* "For where the truth is, the symbol should be put in the background. On other days we consecrate in remembrance of his being sacrificed. But on that day of Good Friday he was veritably sacrificed; for there is no meaning whatever in it when the day comes on which he was actually sacrificed."

separated from the body, that which the body would prevent it from perceiving.

While I was thus contemplating I felt the firmament trembling at the sound of the loudest thunder. An infinite number of heavenly Virtues surrounded the Trinity, then fell down as if in a swoon. The angel then took me and brought me back to the place whence he had taken me. Before restoring its ordinary covering to my soul, he asked me if I had beheld great marvels. "Ah!" I replied, "so great that no tongue could recount them." "Then resume thy body, and now that thou hast no longer any doubts as to the Trinity, go, and receive worthily him whom thou hast learnt to know."

The hermit, thus restored to the possession of his body, no longer saw the angel, but only the book, which he read after he had communicated, and which he laid in the reliquary where was kept the box for the consecrated wafers. He locked the coffer, returned to his *binnacle*, and would not touch the book again until after he had chanted the Easter service. But what were his astonishment and grief when, after the office, he opened the reliquary and found that it was no longer there, though the opening had never been unclosed! Presently a voice spoke these words to him: "Wherefore be surprised that thy book is no longer where thou didst lay it? Did not God come forth from the sepulchre without removing the stone from it? Hearken to what the Great Master doth command thee! To-morrow morning, after chanting mass, thou shalt break thy fast, and then thou shalt take the path leading to the high road. This road will lead thee to that of the *Prise*, near the *Perron*. Thou shalt turn a little aside and take the path towards the right which leads to the cross-roads of the *Eight Paths*, in the plain of *Valestoc*. On reaching the *Fountain of Tears*, where the great slaughter formerly took place, thou wilt find a strange beast commissioned to be thy guide. When thy eyes lose sight of him, thou wilt enter into the land of *Norgave*,* and that will be the end of thy quest.†

This vision is perhaps one of the most spiritual expressions of the Grail legend that can be found, and whoever the hermit was to whom the angel came, or the chronicler who wrote the vision down, the imagination of the person was pure and holy, and the teaching has the ring in it of a high and holy truth.

Yet one more version of this many-leaved book must we glance at before passing on. We have seen the Gnostic Eastern tradition, and the purely Christian, now must be seen the Druidic, or the so-called pagan tradition. Mr. Gould says that there exists a "Red Book," a volume of Welsh prose begun 1318 and finished in 1454, which contains "a Welsh tale entitled Pheredur, which is indisputably the original of Perceval." This book is preserved in the library of Jesus College, Oxford.

Pheredur is mentioned as well in the *Annales Cambriæ*, which extend from the year 444 to 1066.

Mr. Gould says:

Pheredur is not a Christian. His habits are barbarous. The Grail is not a sacred Christian vessel, but a mysterious relic of a past heathen rite.

Taliesin ben Beirdd, the famous poet says: "This vessel inspires poetic genius, gives wisdom, discovers the

---

* I have not discovered a trace of any of these names of places; I am much inclined to think them disguised.

† Paris (A. Paulin), *Romans de la Table Ronde*, i., pp. 156-162. Paris, 1868.

knowledge of futurity, the mysteries of the world, the whole treasure of human sciences."

That this vessel of the liquor of Wisdom held a prominent place in British mythology is certain from the allusions made to it by the bards. Taliesin, in the description of this initiation into the mysteries of the basin, cries out, "I have lost my speech!" because on all who had been admitted to the privileges of full membership secrecy was imposed. This initiation was regarded as a new birth; and those who had once become joined members were regarded as elect, regenerate, separate from the rest of mankind, who lay in darkness and ignorance.

This Druidic mystery was adapted to Christianity by a British hermit A.D. 720. . . . It is likely that the tradition of the ancient druidic brotherhood lingered on and gained consistency again among the Templars. Just as the *Miles Templi* fought for the holy sepulchre, so did the soldier of Montsalvatsch for the Holy Grail. Both orders were vowed to chastity and obedience, both were subject to a head, who exercised regal authority.*

One more link with the ancient Wisdom Religion is forged for us by another author, one perhaps more sympathetic† and he connects the Grail-cult with that Gnostic body named "Mendæens" or the "Christians of St. John";‡ this is a point of extreme interest to

---

* Baring-Gould (S), *Curious Myths of the Middle Ages*, pp. 617, 622-3-4. London, 1881.

† Simrock (R., jr.), *Parzival und Titurel*, p. 776. Stuttgart und Augsberg, 1857.

‡ See Blunt (J. H.), *Dictionary of Sects and Heresies*, p. 309. London, 1874. He says: "An ancient Eastern Sect found in Persia and Arabia, but chiefly at Bussara . . . who profess to be *Mendai-Ijahi* or disciples of St. John the Baptist! They are called 'Christians of St. John' by many European writers, and Sabians or Tzabians by the Mahometans."

students of Theosophy, for it makes a direct connection between the legend of the Holy Grail and the "Order of the Knights Templars," who were so closely allied with this body.

Mackenzie,* moreover, includes the "Johannite Christians," as he terms them, among other bodies connected with Masonry, and indeed many of the Masonic Lodges were dedicated to St. John the Baptist, and looked on him as their patron saint. Simrock builds his theory on the solid fact that Prester John, a mysterious Priest-King of the east (with whom we shall deal next time), was himself a leader of one of the Gnostic sects, a heretic of course; but, as the author points out, the Grail Legend is too intimately interwoven with him for him to be left out. It is to India† indeed, that the Grail goes when the western world becomes too cold for worship, too dead for ideals to stir it to a higher life.

---

* Mackenzie (R. R. H.), *The Royal Masonic Cyclopædia*, p. 386. New York, 1877.

† Weston (Jessie L.), *Parzifal*, ii., notes 184, line 589, p. 223. "The belief in a Christian Kingdom in the east, ruled over by a king who was at the same time a priest, was very widely spread in the middle ages, but it is very curious to find it thus connected with the Grail Legend. Simrock takes this connection to be a confirmation of his theory, that the Grail Myth was originally closely connected with St. John the Baptist. According to *Der Jüngere Titurel*, a poem which, professedly written by Wolfram and long supposed to be his, is now known to be the work of a certain Albert von Scharffenberg, the Grail, with its guardians, Parzival, Lohengrin, Konwiramur, and all the Templars, eventually left Monsalväsch and found a home in the domains of Prester John, but the story seems to be due rather to the imagination of the writer than to any real legendary source."

THE HEAVENLY KINGDOM OF THE HOLY GRAIL.

PART III.

II.
THE HISTORY OF TITUREL.

The fairest of old men ancient whom ever his eyes had seen,
Grey was he as mists of morning.
Parzifal, i. 137, by JESSIE WESTON.

And the Grail, it chooseth strictly, and its Knights must be chaste and pure.—*Ibid.*, i. 283.

To the founding of the Palace Spiritual, and to Titurel, the noble ancestor of the Grail-Kings, our attention must now be turned. Many and varied are the versions which may be found of the history of this Grail-Race, and each interpretation of its traditional history differs according to the writer's sympathy with and comprehension of the mystical history of the human family. Few and far between are those clear-sighted critics who recognize, in this fascinating tradition of Oriental generation, a link which relates the outer life of man to its hidden basis, and sets forth the type of an ideal life which had its inception on this earth when the "Sons of God" still trod its paths, and the "Children of the Fire-mist" had not withdrawn from the outer world, but yet dwelt among the children of men.

From the despised mental dust-bins of the "Dark Middle Ages"—as they are termed—precious gems of rarest literary worth are being disinterred, of quality so pure, with richness so wondrous, that the geniuses of the 19th century show poor and forlorn when measured by the power and mental strength of their predecessors of that despised time. No peers are the modern poets of those noble singers who created the chivalric virtues in the hearts of the men and women of their time, and who sent their burning words ringing through the centuries fraught with love ideals both pure and true, and religious fervour at once self-sacrificing and humble. Their ideals of noble manhood and pure womanhood are still the ideals of the present time, for the "Legend of the Holy Grail" is yet potent, nor can time destroy its "infinite variety." Titurel, the Perfected One, who

> Like a flying star
> Led on the gray-haired Wisdom of the East,

is in modern days deemed to be but the poetical creation of a more than usually fertile-brained troubadour of the Middle Ages; but it is the chronicle of this first spotless Grail-King which must now be studied, for he was the type of the model ruler, pure in life, just in action, living for his people, with his heart set on a higher kingdom than his earthly realm.

The most detailed description of the descent and genealogy of Titurel that we can briefly summarize is given by a group of German authors* in a careful and laborious study of the "Jüngere,"† which runs as follows : Among the princes who gathered round Vespasian at the siege of Jerusalem were Sennabor, a Prince of Cappadocia,‡ and his three sons, Parille, Azubar and Sabbilar. After the fall of the city these three brothers went to Rome, and were overwhelmed with gracious gifts by the Emperor. Parille received his daughter Argusilla § for wife, and some provinces in France were also given to him. To the brothers Azubar and Sabbilar were given Anschowe (Anjou) and Kornwaleis (Cornwall). To Parille and Argusilla was born a son whom they

---

* Hagen (Dr. H. von der), Docen (B. J.), Büsching (J. G.), *Museum für Altdeutsche Literatur und Kunst*, i., 502 *et seq.* Berlin, 1809.

† Scharffenberg (Albrecht von), *Der Jüngere Titurel;* circa 1270. Vilmar (A. F. C.), *Geschichte der deutschen National-Literatur*, i, 147. Marburg u. Leipzig, 1870.

‡ Cappadocia was at this time a Roman Province. Sennabor is rendered by some authorities as "Senbar." Says San Marte: "The first forerunners of Christianity in the west were demigods; and in Asia is rooted the main stem of the Senaboriden. (Bóreaden) Senebar der Reiche—Senber, in Arabic a sage—he came from Cappadocia, from the Caucasus, and Colchis, whence Odin also brought his bloody worship." See "Der Mythus vom Heiligen Gral" in the *Neue Mittheilungen aus dem Gebiet historisch antiquarischer Forschungen.* Herausgegeben von dem Thüringisch-Sächsischen Verein für Erforschung des vaterländischen Alterthums, III., iii., 5.

§ Sometimes given as Orgusille.

named Titurisone, who became the stem of the Grail-Race. Parille tried to reform and Christianize his pagan provinces, which had fallen into degraded superstitions, but he was poisoned by the people and Titurisone reigned in his place.

He married Elizabel of Arragonia, and the royal couple went on a pilgrimage to Jerusalem. There it was they received the prophecy about the great future of the son who should be born to them. He was to be under the special protection of God, and he would be dowered with great gifts. His name was to be formed from those of his father and mother; thus Titurel was he called, which includes a part of Titurisone and Elizabel. He grew in grace and in "favour with God and man." In him was embodied the true type of the ideal Knight, noble, pure, tender and chivalrous. Such was Titurel, the first Grail-King; and—say some accounts—he conquered the rebellious heathen of Auvergne and Navarre, with the help of the Provençals, and the people of Arles and Lotheringen. These combined forces—so runs the tradition—conquered the Saracenic union, and put down the degraded remnants of the old Druidical worship. It was after these long struggles were completed that Titurel was bidden to prepare and build the Temple for the reception of the Holy Grail—that perfect treasure which was to be entrusted to his charge. Amongst the "powers" and "gifts" with which Titurel was dowered was that of "length of days," for when the temple was builded, and he was commanded to marry, in order that the Grail-Race might be continued, Titurel had reached four hundred years of age. The site where the sacred Shrine, or Grail-Temple, was to be founded was shown to him by an angel-guide; so carefully secluded was the spot, that it could not be discovered but by the aid of a higher Power.

It is without doubt on the far side of Pyrenees* that we find this legend most deeply engrafted, though the name of its abiding place is differently rendered by various writers. Thus the name *Mon Salväsch*,† or *Mont Salvat*, may from its wild and inaccessible position only mean the uncultivated mountain, *Mont Salvatge* or *Sauvage*. It is said that between Navarre and Arragon there is still a place named Salvaterra.

The site of the Temple was shown to Titurel, and the "Invisible Helpers" brought him materials for the building; the description is marvellously elaborate, full of symbolical detail,‡ entirely oriental in its whole construction, both material and ideal, but it cannot here be given, as our sketch is limited to

---

* Says Görres: "The Temple of *Mont Salvatsch* stands in Salvatierra, and not as people thought in distant Gallizein, but in Arragonia just at the entrance into Spain, and close to the Valley of Ronceval and the great road which leads from France towards Gallicia and Compostella."—*Lohengrin.* Koblentz, 1812.

† Sometimes called *San-Salvador*, or *Salvez*.

‡ See Boisserée (Sulpiz), *Über die Beschreibung des Heiligen Grals.* Munich, 1834. Also *Transactions of the Munich Academy*, i. 30. The description is in the *Jüngere Titurel*, edited by Hahn, strophe 311, 1842. San Marte (A. Schulz), *Leben und Dichten Wolfram's von Eschenbach*, ii., 357. Magdeburg, 1836.

THE HOLY GRAIL.

Titurel himself. When the building of the Temple was completed he was four hundred years old, but such was the power of the Holy Grail that he looked — says the tradition — only forty. And now he gathered around himself that goodly company of knights—the Knights of the Temple Holy—and gradually their influence and their power spread into other lands; first Arragon and then Navarre were drawn to this spiritual society, then followed Catalonia, Grenada and Gallicia; the chief town of this great alliance was concealed in the forests on the boundaries between Navarre and Arragon, on the ridge of the Pyrenees. The centre of the spiritual supremacy of the new faith reached from Gallicia beyond Provence, towards Burgundy and Lorraine. All of this was done during the four hundred years of Titurel's reign. San Marte speaks of it as a "similar institution to that which existed in the Pythagorean Alliance."

The Sacred Grail was enshrined in the Temple, and the instructions to the King and his knights appeared on its surface, remained there for a while, then faded slowly away. And now was given the order for Titurel to marry, and the wife chosen for him was Richonde, a maiden consecrated to God. Her father's name was Frimutelle, a king of a Spanish province; messengers were sent to her, and she came to Mon Salvatsch accompanied by a great suite of maidens and of warriors, all of whom returned to Spain except those whom the Grail ordered to remain. Titurel had to select two hundred knights from amongst those who came; moral qualifications alone fitted them to enter the service of the Grail. Two children were born to Titurel. His son Frimutel, who married the daughter of the King of Grenat, became the next Grail-King, and they had five children—Amfortas, who succeeded him as Grail-King; Herzeloide, the mother of Parzival; Treverizent, the hermit; Tchoysiane, and Urepanse. This was the male line. The daughter of Titurel married Kailet, King of Spain, the capital of which was, at this time, Toledo, and this marriage connected the Kings of Spain with the Kings of the Grail-Race. It must be remembered that it was at Toledo that the manuscript on the Holy Grail legend was found by Flegetanis, the contents of which gave the Eastern sources of this tradition.

By daily contemplation of the Grail Titurel's life* had been prolonged for five hundred years, and when he knew his forces were beginning to fail him, he gathered his children round him to instruct them on the spiritual significance of the Holy Grail.

Thus he taught: no one may ever see the Grail but the elect; those who do not live a holy life, and guard themselves in purity and from all strife, are not fit to gaze upon that holiness; no tongue may ever tell the Grail's true form.

---

* In Persian history the life of Jemshad was extended to nearly seven centuries from a similar cause.

Titurel also instructed his knights as to the inner meaning of the symbols and ceremonial they used, particularly the spiritual significance and power of the twelve precious stones. He sorrowed that his son Frimutelle had not been "called" by the Grail to be the Grail-King. Shortly after this, we are told, the name of Frimutelle appeared on the Grail, and then followed the names of the Knights who were to enter the Grail service. Titurel was also warned that his son, and his grandson, Amfortas, would suffer bodily injuries, as the result of their ungoverned natures. Finally, Titurel died in India, more than five hundred years old.* Of his journey thither we know nothing, but the tradition runs, that there is a "waiting place,"† whence the return of these knightly souls is expected, in that region of peace, where they dwell and watch over the human race. Thus passes the Founder of the Grail-Kingship from our immediate view; he had but to strike the keynote of a higher purity and a nobler manhood, and his work in the material world of that period ended.

He still holds, we are told, communication with the

---

* One of the few definite dates is given to us by Görres in his *Lohengrin*, p. lxiii. where, speaking of Lohengrin's death, he says: "It was known now to the murderers who this Prince was . . . . they became monks . . . these events took place five hundred years after the birth of Jesus Christ."

† Here we have a clear and most definite hint given that the doctrine of re-incarnation was taught by this Troubadour, who is handing down the Secret Wisdom of the Holy Grail.

world, and occasionally despatches a faithful champion to grant assistance in cases of momentous need. There also the Grail maintains the sanctity of its character, and becomes at once the register of human grievances and necessities, and the interpreter of the will of heaven as to the best mode of redressing them.

Immense stress is laid on the necessity for a perfect purity, but so corrupt did the court grow, that at one time only the infant children of Perceval and Lancelot, and the daughter of Gawain, were considered worthy to step within the sacred shrine.

Warton speaks quite frankly in his book of "esoteric doctrines" which belonged to the "heathen world" (*sic*), and which have been transplanted into Christendom, a new name having therein been given to the old teachings of the East.*

But we must pass on to the other aspects of this legend, and one of the most curious is the connection traced by many authors between the Holy Grail and the traditions of the Knights Templars.†

---

* Warton (Thomas, B.D.), *The History of English Poetry*, i., 85, London, 1824.

† " Le Temple du Graal une fois bâti dans les Pyrénées, Titurel institua pour sa defense et pour sa garde une milice, une Chevalerie spéciale, qui se nomme la Chevalerie du Temple, et dont les membres prennent le nom de Templiens, ou de Templiers. Ces Chevaliers font vœu de chasteté, et sont tenus à une grande pureté de sentimens et de conduite. L'objet de leur vie, c'est de défendre le Graal, ou pour mieux dire, la foi chrétienne, dont ce vase est le symbole, contre les infidèles. Je l'ai déjà insinué, et je puis ici l'affirmer expressément, il y a dans cette milice religieuse du Graal une allusion manifeste à la milice des Templiers. Le but, le caractère religieux, le nom, tout se rapporte entre cette dernière Chevalerie et la Chevalerie idéale du Graal : et l'on

THE HOLY GRAIL.

Aroux is very definite on this point:

"It must be acknowledged," says he, "that the romances of the Sangreal (the legend of which is borrowed from the Apocryphal Gospels) composed, according to an essentially Albigensian idea, in glorification of the Templars, mark the period when the poets of the South felt the need of procuring auxiliaries in the North."[*]

It is Aroux to whom we are chiefly indebted for the secret thread which guides us through much of the tangled maze of the struggles of the mystics during the Middle Ages. He points out that the Holy Grail was a mystic Gospel[†] as well as the Holy Chalice, containing a mysterious power. Another German[‡] thinker connects the legend of Titurel with the origin of the Masonic Orders, and the early *Ritter-Orden* in Germany. It is Herr Doctor Simrock who has given us much detail with regard to the tradition of the Holy Grail and its connection with the "Order of the Knights Templars"; it is his view, and that of other serious students, that that Holy Grail tradition, which is termed by Aroux the "book of the Gospels," was in reality the Secret Doctrine of the Templars, for which they suffered so bitterly.

---

a quelque peine à comprendre la fiction de celle-ci, si l'on fait abstraction de l'existence réelle de l'autre." Fauriel (C.), "Romans Provençaux," *Revue des Deux Mondes;* Première série, viii. 185. Paris, 1832.

[*] Aroux (E.), *La Comédie de Dante,* i. 39. Paris, 1857.

[†] Aroux (E.), *Les Mystères de la Chevalerie,* p. 166. Paris, 1858.

[‡] Rosenkranz (Karl), Doctor der Philosophie, zu Halle. *Uber den Titurel und Dante's Komödie mit einer Vorerinnerung über die Bildung der Geistlichen Ritter-Orden,* pp. 52-70. Halle u. Leipzig, 1829.

Founded in 1118 on the base of the old Society of the Magian Brothers, drawn together by the same guiding powers, the Templars did but develop the ideal seed which Titurel had sown. Let us see what Simrock says on these points.

It seems our duty to bring forward here that which has already been shown to hold good as regards this view. Fauriel, who finds in the *Templeisenthum*—or the Knighthood of the Grail—that there is only a play on the Knights Templars, appeals to the evidence given by the power and the riches which that Order had already obtained in Southern France and the South-East of Spain, but especially in the Pyrenees, where since the founding of the Temple-lands as the first in Europe, by Roger III. Graf von Foix, castles, churches, temples, and chapels had rapidly increased. San Marte lays stress on the agreement of the name as well as on the different rules and customs of the Order which coincided [with those of the Grail]: for instance the Templars at the Lord's Supper, diverging from the Roman Liturgy, made use of the opening words of the Gospel of St. John, which change also occurs at the baptism of Feirefis;* but he bases his arguments chiefly upon the heresies of which the Templars are known to have been accused: the worship of certain idols . . . their belief in spirits and demons, which recall the "Heavenly Host" [around the Grail]—angels who, according to Trevrezent's statement had to serve the Grail as they

---

* Baptism had a much deeper meaning among the Gnostic sects than among the orthodox church people. A "true baptism is only that which takes place in the *living* water;" and again, speaking of S. John the Baptist, "He . . . baptised with the living baptism and named the Name of Life." Brandt (A. J. H. W.), *Die Mandäische Religion, ihre Entwickelung und Geschichtliche Bedeutung*, pp. 98 and 100. Leipzig, 1889. It was an Initiation into the Real Mysteries, and is so still.

hovered around it. The fact remains, however undecided [to San Marte] whether the accusers took their incriminating charges from the Romances of the Grail, or from the scraps which had been published of the real teachings of the Templars.* Other authorities † think that by these Templeisen are to be understood the Knights of San Salvador de Mont Real, who were, however, founded at a much later date, in the year 1120. Another Knightly

---

* Simrock (K. Dr.), *Parzifal und Titurel, Rittergedichte von Wolfram von Eschenbach*, p. 793, third edition. Stuttgart u. Augsburg, 1857.

† Hagen (Dr. H. von der), Docen (B. J.), Büsching (J. G.), *Museum für Altdeutsche Literatur und Kunst*; i., 507. Berlin, 1809. Shallow J. (J. Y. A. Morshead), *The Templer's Trials*, p. 62. London, 1888. "M. Loiseleur considers that the Temple compiled its heresy from the principles of three contemporary sects—Bogomiles, Euchetes, Luciferians. The actual history of these sects, however, rather gives one the impression that each was suggested to some heresiarch by some particular phase of that Manichæan feeling which always existed in Bulgaria or Asia Minor." Mignard (*Monographie du Coffret de M. le Duc de Blacas*, Paris, 1852), proves that the Templars were Cathari—another name for Albigenses—who believed in the doctrine of reincarnation. Says Aroux: "How did Walther of Aquitaine, how did the romance of Perceval, the Perfect Knight of the Saint-Graal, accurately translated by a Templar—Wolfram von Eschenbach, after the poem of the Troubadour Guiot—become transplanted into Germany, if the Provençal missionaries had no relations with that country, if their romances, their symbols were not understood there? .... Who but themselves and their disciples conveyed thither the ideas and romances of chivalry, and by turning to account the national traditions, worked on the foundation of the ancient sagas and impressed on the modern ones the very visible stamp of Albigensianism? Traces are again to be found not only in Europe, but even as far as Asia. True Knights errant of the Church Militant, in open war (but more often war secret and hidden) with Roman Catholicism, they journeyed unceasingly .... sometimes they went as bearers of secret messages or were charged with transmitting verbally important information from Prince to Prince." Thus was the secret mystical teaching preserved through the dark ages. Aroux (E.), *Mystères de la Chevalerie*, p. 189. Paris, 1858.

Order was founded at this period, who wore a "five-pointed star" upon their breasts; they were the Knights of Monfrac in Castille and Knights of Mongoia, on Mont Gaudii in Catalonia. There had, moreover, been a close connection between the Order of the Templars and the House of Anjou, for a tax on his dominions for the benefit of the Templars had been imposed by Fulk. V. of Anjou, on his return from Jerusalem in 1120. It is, however the learned Baron von Hammer-Purgestall* who gives the most detail on the connection of the Templars with the Holy Grail, by tracing its history from the identity of hieroglyphs which he found on the old churches and buildings in the Danubian Provinces. He unfortunately is for ever trying to find the most unsavoury interpretation for all the ancient symbolism; with his views we are not concerned, but to the work of research which he carried on with such ability we are profoundly indebted. His statement is very decided, for on p. 88, in note 33, of his article, he says: The whole poem T8 Titurel, is nothing but the allegory of the Society and the doctrines of the Templars.

Upon these details we cannot dwell, for we must trace the passing of the Holy Grail to India, and this will bring to view another mysterious personage, whose name was Prestre John—a man about whom legends were rife in both East and West during the early Middle Ages. Colonel Yule speaks of his history as

* Hammer-Purgestall (J. Baron von), "Mysterium Baphometis Revelatum; seu fratres militiæ Templi, quâ Gnostici et quidem ophiani, apostasiæ, idololatriæ et quidem impuritatis convicti per ipsa eorum monumenta." See *Fundgruben des Orients*, vi. p. 3. Vienna, 1818. Nell (M. von) writing on Hammer's "Baphometum," says that Hammer insists that the Cup of the Holy Graal is Gnostic, and of the same set as the Baphometo of the Templars, which all have Gnostic-Ophite symbols on them. But Nell says they are theosophical and alchemical: in both cases these authors trace the Grail legend to heretical sects.

"that of a phantom taking many forms."* The so-called apostate Nestorians, and the personage called Presbyter Johannes, appear to have been Manichæan Buddhists; the country of Prestre John was Indian Tartary, and the real Prestre John was the Grand Lama, the incarnation of Wisdom or Gnyâna.† Every authority joins in admitting that there was some mysterious and powerful individual of this name, some identifying him with Gengis-Khan.‡

---

* Yule (Col.): see *sub voce*, *Encyclo. Brit.*

† "Prestre John" seems to have been the title of an office, for the periods of time at which we hear of this curious person are various. The person who succeeded to the position took the designation Prestre John.

‡ Sir John Maundeville, an old knight, writing in the fourteenth century, relates (Cassell's National Library, *The Voyages and Travels of Sir John Maundeville*, p. 169) the following: "This Emperor Prester John takes always to wife the daughter of the great Chan, and the great Chan also in the same wise the daughter of Prester John. For they two are the greatest lords under the firmament. . . . And Prester John has under him seventy-two provinces, and in every province is a king, all which kings are tributary to Prester John, and in his lordships are many great marvels, for in his country is the sea called the Gravelly Sea. . . . Three days from that sea are great mountains, out of which runs a great river which comes from Paradise, and it is full of precious stones without a drop of water. . . . Beyond that river is a great plain, and in that plain every day at sunrise small trees begin to grow, and they grow till midday, bearing fruit; but no man dare take of that fruit, for it is a thing of fairie. . . . This Emperor Prester John when he goes to battle against any other lord has no banners borne before him, but he has three large crosses of gold full of precious stones, and each cross is set in a chariot full richly arrayed. . . . And when he has no war but rides with a private company, he has before him but one plain cross of wood, in remembrance that Jesus Christ suffered death upon a wooden cross. And they carry before him also a platter of gold full of earth, in token that his nobleness and his might and his flesh shall turn to earth. And he has borne before him also a vessel of silver, full of noble jewels of gold

We must now return to the Grail Legend and trace the connection which is therein made between this cryptic entity and that tradition.

"The passage of the Grail to India," says San Marte, "and the transformation of Parzival into Prestre John is important for us to notice; according to the version of Wolfram, this curious and interesting person is the son of Urepanse,* hence a cousin of Parzival; no details are given to us about this mysterious personage, whose existence, however, cannot be denied. The Monk Wilhelm von Rubruquis,† passing through the East about 1253, told of a ruler in the northern regions of India, in 1057, called Ken-Khan. The Turks sought his help against the Christians. The Nestorians called him King Johannes. Interior Asia was peopled by numerous sects; besides the Nestorians were the Jacobites, Monophysites, and the Zaböer or Johannes Christians. All travellers of the thirteenth

---

and precious stones, in token of his lordship, nobility and power . . . the frame of his bed is of fine sapphires, blended with gold to make him sleep well. This Emperor Prester John has evermore seven kings with him to serve him, who share their service by certain months."

* Urepanse was one of the grand-daughters of Titurel.

† In the account of the travels of Rubruquis, in the *Geography of the Middle Ages*, Book III., p. 270, London, 1831, we read: "There is reason to believe that the Nestorians had penetrated into China as early as the sixth or seventh century, and carried into that kingdom the civilization of the Bactrian Greeks." Rubruquis says, that in his time they "inhabited fifteen cities in Cathay. . . . The Nestorians of Tartary had imbibed the specious doctrine of the transmigration of souls." They then told him of a child about three years old who could write and reason, and who stated "that he had passed through three several bodies." William de Rubruquis—or more properly, Van Ruysbroek—was a Minorite Friar, from a village of that name near Brussels. He started on his travels in 1253. He also said (p. 273), "that he had been told by Baldwin de Hainault at Constantinople some facts about the direction of the rivers in Tartary which he afterwards found to be true."

century speak of a widely-spread Christianity in the East, and the information thereof may have come to the West with the first crusade—confused with vague intelligence about the Hierarchy of the Dalai Lama, of whom Kiot may have heard."*

Writing on the "Disciples of St. John," Madame Blavatsky† says:

Glancing rapidly at the Ophites and Nazareans, we shall pass to their scions which yet exist in Syria and Palestine, under the name of Druzes of Mount Lebanon; and near Basra or Bassorah, in Persia, under that of Mendaeans, or Disciples of St. John. All these sects have an immediate connection with our subject, for they are of kabalistic parentage and have once held to the secret "Wisdom-Religion," recognizing as the One Supreme, the Mystery-God of the *Ineffable Name*. Noticing these numerous secret societies of the past, we will bring them into direct comparison with several of the modern.

Our object is not to write the history of either of them; but only to compare these sorely-abused communities with the Christian sects, past and present, and then, taking historical facts for our guidance, to defend the secret science as well as the men who are its students and champions against any unjust imputation.

One by one the tide of time engulfed the sects of the early centuries, until of the whole number only one survived in its primitive integrity. That one still exists, still teaches the doctrine of its founder, still exemplifies its faith in works of power. The quicksands which swallowed up every other outgrowth of the religious agitation of the times

---

* *Neue Mittheilungen aus dem Gebiete Historisch-Antiquarischer Forschungen*, ii. 36.

† Blavatsky (H. P.), *Isis Unveiled*, ii.; pp. 289, 290. New York, 1884.

of Jesus, with its records, relics, and traditions, proved firm ground for this. Driven from their native land, its members found refuge in Persia, and to-day the anxious traveller may converse with the direct descendants of the "Disciples of John," who listened, on the Jordan's shore, to the "man sent from God," and were baptized and believed. This curious people, numbering thirty thousand or more, are mis-called "Christians of St. John," but, in fact, should be known by their old name of Nazareans, or their new one of Mendaeans.

The poem entitled *Der Jüngere Titurel** deals most minutely with the passing of the Grail-Kings to the realms of Prestre John ; and in this work it is not Parzival around whom the chief interest is grouped, but Titurel and his race, as they follow the Founder ; then—when the darkening of the spiritual fervour begins, and the falling away from the standard of purity grows more general—then with prayer and fasting do the few sorrowing knightly souls, the Templeisen, make preparations to return to that east whence had come their early inspiration. Led by Parzival they pass from West to East. The description of the kingdom of Prestre John far surpasses, however, in splendour that of the Holy Grail. There, we are told, the whole of nature is sanctified ; it is a land free from crime, perfidy, scoffing, and lack of faith.

Prestre John is described as a man holy before God and man, perfect in virtue, and glorified with

---

* Scharffenberg (A. von), *Der Jüngere Titurel*, 1270, line 5893 *et seq.*

humility: he gives honour to Parzival, who comes bringing the Holy Grail to its Indian home, and the Priest-King of that land offers his crown and kingdom to the king of the Grail-Race; Parzival desires, in his humility, to give himself to the service of Prestre John, and finally it is the Grail which decides the noble strife of these two great souls. The decree was given that Parzival should accept the kingship, but his name was to be changed into that of Prestre John.

Then was fulfilled a prophecy, formerly made by an angel, that Prestre John should receive a son who should be a more powerful ruler than himself. But it was also decreed that Parzival should only wear the crown for ten years, since he was not entirely purified from the sin that his mother, Herzeloide, had died of grief for him. As San Marte* points out, the sin was entirely unintentional on his part; nevertheless, it was still unexpiated and stained that spotless purity of a perfect life which was demanded of every knight who entered the service of the Holy Grail. Thus it appears that even a more perfect condition was required in the office of the Priest-King Johannes

---

* San Marte (A. Schulz), "Vergleichung von Wolfram's Parzival mit Albrecht's Titurel in Theologischer Beziehung," *Germania*, viii., 454. Wien, 1863. This writer also remarks in the same interesting article that "the poem appears as a mirror of those religious movements at the end of the twelfth century which were struggling towards freedom from the compulsion of the Church . . . . the fundamental appreciation of both poems, 'Titurel' and 'Parzival,' is only obtained by comparing them from the theological standpoint. . . . Titurel is full of learned and varied reminiscences brought from afar." *Op. cit. supra*, pp. 421, 422.

than in that of the Grail-Kingship. The holders of both offices were nominated by the Holy Grail.

III.

THE LINKS OF THE MYSTIC CHAIN.

The strongly Eastern tinge that characterises this tradition may be noticed in many different points. The knowledge, for instance, of the occult properties of precious stones and metals and their powers; the stone that enables the wearer to make himself invisible, the condition being that he should do nothing dishonourable. Then we have the mysterious land of mist, where people* are neither dark nor light, but have lost all ordinary human colour. Again, there is the magic column brought from India, in which all that happens for miles around is represented; and one of the most important links is the clear reference made to reincarnation in the belief held that Titurel and his knights may return, and that the Perfect King still holds communication with the earth and its sorrows.

The moral and mystic teaching of the Grail tradition is the most vitally interesting to the student of Theosophy and mysticism, for the resemblances between the present laws of spiritual development and those given to the Knights of the Grail are strikingly identical: The knight who watched

---

* Some of the Kâmalokic planes might be thus described.

the Grail—the highest office—had to be entirely pure; all sensual love, even within the bounds of marriage, was forbidden; one single thought* of passion would obscure the eye and conceal the mystic vessel; the only marriage that was permitted amongst those who stepped on to this "Path" was the marriage of the King, and even that was not based on personal attractions or attachments; the Grail alone decided whom the Grail-King should take as wife. Not for himself, not for gratification, but for the service of the race was he to marry.

As we search into the mystic chalice symbolism of the Grail myth does it not become clear that we are face to face with a symbol of man: man who is the temple of the Holy Spirit. The chalice or cup is but another way of denoting the "coats of skin," the "veils" or "vestures" which garment man on earth; robes woven by the nature powers, in which and through which the divine spark has to dwell, until in process of time the vestures or chalice become permeated through and through by the divine light within. Says one writer on this subject:

"In that marvellous relic of Gnostic philosophy called the *Pistis-Sophia*, the three vestures of the Glorified Christos or perfected man—what we may all be in some future birth—are thus described:

"And the disciples saw not Jesus because of the great light with which he was surrounded, or which proceeded

---

* One single thought about the past that thou hast left behind will drag thee down." Blavatsky (H. P.), *The Voice of the Silence*, p. 23. London, 1892.

from him. For their eyes were darkened because of it. But they gazed upon the Light only, shooting forth great rays of light. Nor were the rays equal to one another, and the Light was of divers modes and various aspect, from the lower to the higher part thereof, each ray more admirable than its fellow in infinite manner, in the great radiance of the immeasurable Light. It stretched from the earth to the heaven. . . . It was of three degrees, one surpassing the other in infinite manner. The second, which was in the midst, excelled the first, which was below it, and the third, the most admirable of all, surpassed the other twain."

The Master explains this mystery to his disciples as follows:

"Rejoice, therefore, in that the time is come that I should put on my Vesture.

"Lo! I have put on my Vesture and all power has been given me by the First Mystery. Yet a little while and I will tell you every Mystery and every Completion; henceforth from this hour I will conceal naught from you, but in Perfectness will I perfect you in all Completion, and all Perfectioning and every Mystery, which indeed are the End of all Ends, and the Completion of all Completions, and the Wisdom (Gnosis) of all Wisdoms. Hearken! I will tell you all things which have befallen me.

"It came to pass, when the sun had risen in the places of the East, a great Stream of Light descended, in which was my Vesture."*

The vesture of the Self in its perfect glory is of a purity of transcendent perfection. No mortal stained with earthly passion can gaze upon that garment of the soul.

And as the upward striving soul struggles to free

---

* Mead (G. R. S., B.A.), *The World-Mystery*, pp. 102, 104. London, 1895.

itself from the bondage of the lower bodies and their subtle forces, and as it purifies one vehicle after another pertaining to the three lower planes of matter, finally it reaches that step on the Path whereof the substance is perfect purity, and the soul perceives that "Light vesture" which is the garment —spoken of in theosophic terms as the buddhic body —veiling the divine mysterious Self.

This is the great reality which is typified by the Holy Grail, the symbolic Cup or Chalice, the first container of the Holy Life of the Logos. In all religions is this myth to be found; truly an "outward and visible sign of an inward and spiritual grace." Titurel had told his knights that no tongue may ever tell the Grail's true form. This shows that some mystery was concealed behind the outward symbolism of the Cup and Chalice, or Gospel.

Burnouf says: "In spite of the difference produced by the influences of the place, the study of the legend of the Vase permits us to understand and discover that esoteric teaching which has never ceased to animate or ensoul the five great Aryan religions. This theory—which in the Christian churches was transmitted under the name of the Secret Doctrine, *disciplina secreti*—is of a Fire as the universal force under different names, always the same at the basis, and manifesting itself by the same words and symbols."

This Fire is the true Spirit of life, the living Word,

Burnouf (É.), *Le Vase Sacré et ce qu'il contient : dans l'Inde, la Perse, la Grèce, et dans l'Église Chrétienne;* avec un appendice sur le Saint Graal, p. 172. Paris, 1896.

which inflames the soul of man, and gives it that force by which it can conquer the kingdoms of the lower world, and, crossing the ocean of births and deaths, can finally land itself on the further shore, a holy, purified "Son of God," a Saviour of Worlds to come.

Thus runs the Legend of the Holy Grail.